T0340527

COMFORT IN DARKNESS

COMFORT
IN DARKNESS

THE INVISIBLE POWER OF JIU JITSU

Rickson Gracie

WITH PETER MAGUIRE

HarperCollins*Publishers*

HarperCollins*Publishers*
1 London Bridge Street
London SE1 9GF

www.harpercollins.co.uk

HarperCollins*Publishers*
Macken House, 39/40 Mayor Street Upper
Dublin 1, D01 C9W8, Ireland

First published by HarperCollins*Publishers* 2024

10 9 8 7 6 5 4 3 2 1

Designed by Alison Bloomer
Illustrations by Chris Burns

A catalogue record of this book is
available from the British Library

HB ISBN 978-0-00-872516-7
PB ISBN 978-0-00-872517-4

Printed and bound in the UK using 100% renewable
electricity at CPI Group (UK) Ltd

This book is produced from independently certified FSC™ paper
to ensure responsible forest management.

For more information visit: www.harpercollins.co.uk/green

To my wife, Cassia, and my children, Rockson, Kaulin, Kauan, and Kron

CONTENTS

THE RICKSON GRACIE DIALECTIC

BY PETER MAGUIRE

TODAY, THE PHRASE "MIXED MARTIAL ARTS" (MMA) CONJURES IMAGES OF HEAVILY tattooed, steroid-swollen monsters pounding each other bloody and senseless in metal cages to the blaring sounds of heavy metal music before a global television audience. Although Rickson Gracie, arguably the greatest MMA fighter of the twentieth century, looks and carries himself more like a Latin American aristocrat than an MMA *Übermensch*, the Ultimate Fighting Championship (UFC) is his family's creation and grew out of the martial art they invented.

Gracie is regularly compared to sports greats like basketball player Michael Jordan or hockey player Wayne Gretzky, but a more accurate analogy may be dancer Rudolf Nureyev, the bullfighter Manolete, or Chessmaster Garry Kasparov. After American wrestling legend and Olympic gold medalist Mark Schultz (*Foxcatcher*) lost twice to Gracie in a private match, he said simply, "Rickson was the best fighter I'd ever seen." Although Rickson Gracie's three decades of total dominance in competition Jiu Jitsu and bare-knuckle *vale tudo* (the much tougher antecedent to MMA) fighting is astounding, even more astounding is the serenity and spiritual depth of his approach to hand-to-hand combat.

Gracie's relationship with martial arts is more of an example of Friedrich Nietzsche's "happy/gay science" (*die fröhliche Wissenschaft*) than it is a vindication of the UFC's American entrepreneurial dream. His training regimen is neither solemn, nor self-important, nor exhibitionistic; rather, it is playful, flexible, and even lighthearted. When Gracie exercises, he does not count sets, much less watch the clock; instead, he tries to reach a state where he feels a balance between his mind, body, and spirit.

For Rickson Gracie, his art is not a sport; it is a philosophical practice. To him, the most interesting aspects of martial arts are not the techniques, but the invisible elements—the ever-changing senses of touch, weight, and momentum. His explanations of Jiu Jitsu are reminiscent of Zen Buddhist Takuan Soho's description of "immovable wisdom" in swordsmanship or Eugen Herrigel's "unconscious control" in Zen Archery.

Today, the retired champion is no longer interested in MMA or competitive Jiu Jitsu. Instead, he uses his art as a tool to teach students about themselves, a fact I can personally attest to. I first met Rickson Gracie at his now-legendary Pico Academy in the summer of 1992. I was finishing my PhD in history at Columbia University but was in Los Angeles for the summer. For the previous two years, I had been training with a martial artist in New York City who was a physically brilliant autodidact. Long before the UFC, he was teaching a handful of students an early version of mixed martial arts. In addition to holding several black belts in traditional martial arts, our teacher had kickboxed professionally, and fought underground fights in New York City's Chinatown and Long Island's Native American reservations. In a loft in Manhattan, he taught me and a handful of others kickboxing, boxing, Wing Tsun kung fu, grappling, and knife fighting.

After I got my hands on a copy of Rorion Gracie's *Gracie in Action* videotape in 1990, my classmates and I watched it over and over. Before the internet, all of us aspiring martial artists traded fight tapes like religious relics, and none was more prized than *Gracie in Action*. Not only did it introduce us to the Gracies, the first family of Brazilian Jiu Jitsu, but the sight of skinny Brazilians also tackling and choking out kickboxers who were far better than us was eye-opening. This, coupled with Rorion Gracie's provocative mantra that "all fights end up on the ground," planted seeds of doubt in my mind about my reliance on punching and kicking.

During the summer of 1992, a wrestler friend told me that Rickson, the greatest Gracie, had opened a school in West LA. I asked him to try to get me a private lesson and much to my surprise, he called a day later and said, "Be there at two. Rickson's school is a little hard to find. Go east on Pico. When you hit Sepulveda, look for a fabric store on your right. Park when you see it, then walk down the driveway to the back of the building. Oh yeah," he added as an afterthought. "They wanted to know if this is a lesson or a challenge." I told him it was just a lesson. "Make sure to remind them when you get there. Lots of guys are showing up at his school to fight."

The next day, I drove down Pico until I saw H. Rimmon Fabrics on my right, then pulled over and parked. I walked down the driveway, past an auto body shop, and saw a set of swinging, saloon-style doors. I pushed them open and entered a starkly lit, traditional Japanese karate school with a raised wooden platform, a *makiwara*, and an oil painting of an old Japanese karate master on the wall. While the sign said "West LA Karate," something was amiss. The platform was covered with frayed green wrestling mats, and there were tan, fit

Latinos sleeping on them. The West LA Karate School had rented their facility to Rickson and now this nondescript fighters' gym was ground zero for a coming martial arts revolution that would forever change the way that the world looked at fighting.

"Can I help you?" asked the short, smiling man with a thick Brazilian accent and ghoulishly disfigured cauliflower ears, sitting at a desk and eating a late lunch.

"Yes, I'm here for a private," I replied to Rickson's master sergeant, Luis "Limão" Heredia.

"Rickson's on his way," he said, then returned to his lunch. I changed in the tiny locker room, and when I began to warm up by kicking the heavy bag, Limão got up from his desk, walked over, and asked casually, "Are you here for a lesson or a challenge?" His expression did not change when I replied "Lesson," because the "Gracie Challenge" was a fact of his life.

Revolutions are won by force, not words. An important part of the Gracie ethos was, and remains, the "Gracie Challenge." To prove the effectiveness of their fighting system, the brothers openly challenged other fighters from all styles to test their skills against Jiu Jitsu in as real a fight as they desired. The challenge could be a sporting affair that a tap on the ground at any time would end, but other matches were *vale tudo*, Portuguese for "anything goes." In these fights, there were no gloves, or short rounds, and only two rules: no biting or eye-gouging. Unlike America's much tamer UFC, in *vale tudo*, headbutts, elbows, and knees on the ground were all perfectly legal.

Compared to Asian martial arts, Gracie Jiu Jitsu was informal. There were only five belts—white, blue, purple, brown, and black—and the only way to get promoted was by defeating higher belts. While Rickson would theoretically fight a challenge, a contender first had to make it through his platoon of incredibly tough blue, purple, and brown belts. The challenges were usually formal and respectful affairs but could quickly degenerate into beatings if someone broke the social contract by biting, eye-gouging, or any other form of unsportsman-like conduct. Those who violated the social contract, I quickly became aware, were severely handled here.

Twenty minutes late, Rickson walked in, smiled at me, and apologized for his tardiness. When he shook my hand, he looked deeply into my eyes, then began to feel my shoulders, triceps, and lats, taking in nonverbal clues about me. In a nanosecond, he knew that I was as harmless to him as a gnat. Gracie was not tall, but he was extremely broad-shouldered. What struck me the most was how thick he was from his back to his chest.

Having grown accustomed to a more brutal martial arts pedagogy, my first lesson with Rickson was surprisingly calm and theoretical. First, he asked me to get into a fighting stance, then he checked my "base" by pushing, then pulling me. As the lesson went on, I was struck by how academic my first class was. Rickson's dialectic explored physical problems that he described in terms like "base," "engagement," "connection," "leverage," and "timing."

While grapplers had always impressed me, I detested robotic martial arts drills, whether it was wrestling, Judo, or kung fu. Gracie's approach to grappling was the opposite. It was totally intuitive and relied as heavily on the senses as it did the brain or the body. By the end of that first hour, Rickson made an instant believer out of me, because he had challenged my intellect instead of my ego. I examined and attempted to solve the physical problems he posed, and my answers were either validated or refuted by a physical trial and error on the mat. Toward the end of the lesson, he asked me to try to pin him in any position I wanted, then he escaped with little or no effort. Next, Rickson told me to try to slap him, tied me in a knot in seconds, and the only evidence of his effort was his loud, rhythmic exhalations.

As I was getting ready to leave, Gracie's frontline soldiers were filing in, licking their wounds, and psyching up for the evening class. Both Brazilian and American, the Pico Academy's first generation of students were the guys who took on all challengers. The Brazilians were led by Luis Limão, Mauricio Costa, Luis Claudio, Coyote, Fernando "Dentinho" Fayzano, and a revolving cast of *carioca* cousins and friends. The Americans were equally impressive: Chris Saunders, Mark Ekerd, David Kama, Stefanos Miltsakakis, and the dangerous teenager, Richard "Hicky" Hillman. It was clear that each one of these guys would have taken a bullet for Rickson, so the formal and informal challenge matches were cherished opportunities to carry the Gracie flag.

Before I left the Pico Academy that day, Rickson invited me to come back and train seriously when I had more time. I returned to LA the next summer, and instead of private lessons, I attended his 10:30 a.m. "Men's Open Class." Many of my classmates were professional fighters and martial artists like MMA pioneer Erik Paulson, martial artist and Navy SEAL hand-to-hand combat instructor Paul Vunak, and fellow white belt John Lewis, who would go on to fight in the UFC. While Paulson and Lewis were incredibly fit, game, and athletic fighters, much more daunting were the professional dangerous guys like the slightly fat, grizzly bear-like prison guard and the offshore oil rig roughneck whose hands were the size of catchers' mitts. These men were a different species. It did not matter how slow they were or how obviously they telegraphed their moves; their size and strength allowed them to take what they wanted. Hawaiian big-wave surfer Leonard Brady best captured the mood: "At the end of my privates with Rickson Gracie at his classic Pico Academy, the group class would fill in—everyone shirts off, heavy attitudes, heavily tattooed—total prison yard at workout time."

Socially, the class was divided into fighters that surfed, surfers that fought, and nonsurfing fighters. The Brazilians all surfed, and skill in the water was as important to them as skill on the mats. Luckily, I was a lifelong surfer and traveled the world to surf some of the world's most challenging waves. This put me in good stead with the Brazilians, as did my access to many of California's secret and private surf spots.

One constant at the Pico Academy that summer was the Brazilian chorus. Like a Greek chorus, it could be happy, sad, angry, or spiteful. The first time I became aware of it was when a pretty Brazilian girl burst through the academy's swinging doors speaking loudly and excitedly in Portuguese about a bodybuilder at her gym who had talked disparagingly about her Gracie Jiu Jitsu T-shirt. Instantly, my classmates' dark eyes narrowed, and their expressions changed. After a thirty-second cross-examination, four Brazilians, one armed with a video camera, piled into her VW Rabbit and tore out of the parking lot to find the bodybuilder. Forty-five minutes later, they returned, laughing, and although they did not find their prey, they left a standing invitation for him at his gym to come visit the Pico Academy anytime.

One day Rickson told us to line up against the wall and began to talk in an honest and open way about nerves and fear. I wondered why everyone suddenly got so tense and nervous. I immediately understood when Rickson pointed to his left and said, "One hundred sixty pounds and above," then to his right and said, "One sixty and under." This would be my first interclass tournament. These regular informal competitions kept everybody honest about their place in the Pico Academy's food chain. Because Rickson was the matchmaker and referee, the hierarchy at the Pico Academy was a natural one.

I drew a lanky Brazilian blue belt in my first match. I aggressively rushed in for a takedown, and after a brief scramble, we were on the ground. Although I was on top of him, he had wrapped his legs around my waist in the classic Gracie Jiu Jitsu guard. As the Brazilian grabbed my wrist with one hand and my tricep with the other, his loose hips swung. Suddenly, the back of a powerful thigh hit me in the face, found a comfortable home under my chin, and began to separate my head from my arm. Intent on not tapping out, I tried to pull away, but this only tightened his lock on my arm. As the pressure on my elbow increased, the feelings of tendons straining transformed into an internal sound—like a high-tension cable squealing, then snapping due to pressure. As my elbow hyperextended, I could hear and feel things inside my elbow capsule popping one at a time—"bink-bink-bink."

By the time I tapped, it was way too late, the damage was done, and the injury was my fault. While I tried to mask the pain, I could tell by the sickened looks on the faces of my classmates that they knew I was injured. There was a brief, harsh exchange between my opponent and the Brazilian chorus. I don't speak Portuguese and I had no idea what the words meant, but I knew exactly what they were saying. It went something like this:

CHORUS: "Why did you pop his elbow?"
OPPONENT: "He should have fuckin' tapped."
CHORUS: "Sigh . . . Yes, he should have . . ."

After the class ended, Rickson approached me and upbraided me for my haste and poor technique. Finally, he said, "Next time, *tranquillo*." My arm was not broken, but my elbow was damaged, and for the next six months, every time I paddled a surfboard, I thought of the lanky Brazilian.

Other days, Rickson lined the class up against the wall and took on every single student, one after another. The matches would rarely last more than two or three minutes, but there were usually twenty to thirty of us. He made me tap with a standing armlock in less than thirty seconds.

On still other days, Luis Limão would don a comically large pair of old, worn, leather lace-up boxing gloves and stand in the center of the mats. The exercise was a simple one: you had to tackle Limão before he punched you in the face. Given my background in Wing Tsun and kickboxing, his loopy boxing punches were easy to avoid.

For other students, however, this boxing drill was their worst nightmare. Just as boxers don't understand the spatial relationship between two people grappling on the ground, at that time, Jiu Jitsu fighters did not box. Their sole objective was to get their opponent on the ground, where they were most at home. The worse you were at stand-up fighting, the harder you got hit. Unaccustomed to dodging blows, some of my classmates ate horrible shots, and Limão spared them neither pain nor humiliation. In our teacher's mind, it was better to pay now, behind closed doors in the academy, than out on the streets.

The Brazilians were impressed by my hands, especially Rickson's eleven-year-old son Rockson. Jiu Jitsu's crown prince was still just a skinny boy, but even then it was clear that he had the heart of a lion. He was intent on following in his grandfather's, father's, uncles', and cousins' footsteps. While I liked Rockson and he liked me, I was a native Angeleno and knew all too well what perils came with rising to every challenge in the City of Angels. Rockson was quick to identify weak members of the Pico Academy's herd. He would innocently ask them if he could practice his choke on them. They did not suspect that such small and skinny arms could be capable of such power. Some went unconscious and woke up with a laughing child standing over them.

If the waves weren't good, I trained three days a week and was in the best shape of my life. Many nights I had a hard time sleeping, because the tops of both my ears were throbbing blood blisters. Irrespective of my swollen ears, sore elbow, and bruised body, my Jiu Jitsu was getting exponentially better. In my second interclass tournament, I submitted my first opponent with a choke in less than a minute, then lost a close decision to a second, much larger opponent. After the tournament, I approached Rickson and fished for a compliment: "Better than the last tournament?" Rickson rolled his eyes and sneered, "What do you think?"

Halfway through the summer, Rickson's brother Royce began coming to the Pico Academy to train with him. The rumor in the academy was that Rickson was preparing him to fight in America's first *vale tudo* competition. The Ultimate Fighting Championship was largely the brainchild of the oldest Gracie brother, Rorion. Subsequently it has been claimed that Royce Gracie was selected to represent the family, because he appeared so young and unthreatening. While that might have been partially true, Rickson posed a direct threat to his older brother Rorion's hegemony over Gracie Jiu Jitsu. Nonetheless, for a time, the Gracie brothers put their differences aside to prepare their younger brother for the first UFC. Although Royce was a formidable fighter in his own right, he was not in Rickson's league, and this was obvious when we watched them training in the corner of the mats before our class.

Royce would do his best to endure and survive his brother's unrelenting pressure, but that was all. When Rickson sensed that Royce was close to his breaking point, he would turn up the heat one last time, then end their match playfully. Instead of sinking a choke, he would pat Royce on the head or kiss his cheek, and all of the strain and tension of the past hour would dissipate as they joked and laughed in a way that only brothers can.

Advertised as a human cockfight in order to entice an American audience raised on Bruce Lee movies and the World Wrestling Federation, the UFC was a single-elimination tournament based on traditional Brazilian *vale tudo* rules. There were no gloves, no rounds, no time limits, and the only rules were no biting or eye-gouging. On November 12, 1993, 7,800 spectators attended the first UFC in Denver, Colorado, and another 86,000 paid $14.95 to watch on pay-per-view television.

After Royce submitted a boxer, a wrestler, and a kickboxer to win the first tournament, the popularity of Gracie Jiu Jitsu exploded. When I returned to the Pico Academy in December 1993, it was packed with students, and the mood was triumphant. I had just received my PhD in history from Columbia University, and even though my dissertation on the Nuremberg Trials and the laws of war had received the highest honors, I felt hollow and fraudulent, like a boxing commentator who had never stepped into the ring. I was twenty-eight, a product of the softest generation in American history, and all I knew about conflict was what I had read.

So instead of embarking on my academic career, I volunteered to work for a nonprofit in Cambodia that was documenting Khmer Rouge war crimes. When I told Rickson that I was going to an unstable, war-torn nation to investigate atrocities, he looked at me with curiosity and asked why. I told him that I wanted to find out how the Khmer Rouge had gotten away with genocide, try to hold their leaders accountable, and if nothing else, collect and preserve the evidence of their crimes. He nodded gravely, hugged me, and told me to be careful.

While I was in Asia, Royce defended his UFC title in devastating fashion—three of his four matches did not last a minute. Even though Royce was overshadowing his older brother in America, there was never any confusion about who the best fighter in the family was. In a postfight interview, Royce readily admitted, "Rickson is ten times better than me."

My first investigation centered around Tuol Sleng Prison. In 1976, the Khmer Rouge turned this former high school into a torture and interrogation center. More than twenty thousand people entered, and possibly twenty survived. Early interviews with Khmer Rouge survivors pushed me to the limits of theories of perfect justice that sounded much more convincing in university seminar rooms than in the hot, dusty backstreets of Phnom Penh.

I returned from Southeast Asia in the spring of 1994 and ran into Rickson at sunrise one morning at Malibu's Surfrider Beach. In many ways, I was a changed man. Rickson's life was changing just as fast as mine. He excitedly told me that he had just signed a contract to fight in Japan's first *vale tudo* tournament. He said that he preferred to fight in Japan, because they had a much deeper understanding of martial arts and warrior culture than Americans. Rickson invited me to his house to train before I left LA.

A few days later, I went to his house and brought some of the evidence that I had collected in Cambodia. Rickson winced as he looked at a photograph of a young boy with a padlock and chain around his neck, then a bare-chested young man with the number 17 pinned through the flesh of his chest. When he saw a sad-looking mother whose child's disembodied fist grabbed at her sleeve, he handed me back the stack of 8x10 photographs and asked *Why*. So began a conversation that has continued for almost thirty years.

For the next decade, I devoted myself to holding the Khmer Rouge leaders accountable for their atrocities. My search for witnesses and evidence took me back to Cambodia many times, but also to Vietnam, Thailand, former East Germany, France, the Hague, Washington, D.C., and elsewhere. In addition to investigations, I regularly briefed United Nations, US government, and human rights officials on the unlikely prospect of a Khmer Rouge war crimes trial. During this time, with Rickson's blessings, I also introduced Gracie Jiu Jitsu to Cambodia, proved its efficacy, and converted tough doubters into students and lifelong friends. When Cambodia won their first ever gold medal in the 2020 Asia Games, I was very proud that it was in Jiu Jitsu.

After many of my long and exhausting investigative trips overseas, I would clear customs at LAX, then drive straight to Rickson's house. I would arrive unannounced, still reeking of woodsmoke, dust, and stale sweat. I was eager to sigh a big breath of relief and tell my friend and teacher about my latest discoveries and martial encounters. Often, I would find Rickson in his garage teaching a private lesson to a Jiu Jitsu legend who was in town for a tournament, or standing in a puddle of sweat, strengthening his neck with a homemade elastic contraption, or doing breathing exercises in his unheated swimming pool.

"Fala Champion," he would say with an always-welcoming, but slightly bemused, smile. As he hugged me, like always, he took my measure. Rickson could always sense when I had been running on minimal sleep, adrenaline, coffee, PowerBars, cigarettes, beer, and Valium for weeks on end. Before I could open my briefcase and start my show-and-tell, he would say, "Take off your boots, let's play around a little bit." Sometimes he gave me Gi pants to put on, but most of the time I trained in the same dirty clothes that I had been wearing for days.

What I did not realize until many years later was that Rickson sensed my imbalance, and he was using Jiu Jitsu to slow me down, center me, and pull me back down to earth. These lessons were always long, intense, and built around a single minute detail that he sensed I was missing. He repeated the words "base," "connection," "leverage," and "timing" like mantras until he was convinced that I didn't just know these concepts, I felt them. One time he told me to stand and defend myself and then began to throw open-handed slaps at me. After I blocked and countered all of them, he said, "Yes, your hands work very well." Then, suddenly, he threw a much more powerful haymaker. Although I blocked it, the force of his blow spun me 360 degrees. Rickson laughed and said, "But you are weak because your hands are not connected to your base."

Just as quickly as our impromptu classes would begin, they would end. It was usually when one of his children saw me and wanted to hear about my latest trip. I told them about fighting off attackers on speeding motorcycles, escaping the crush of a stampeding crowd of thousands during Cambodia's annual Water Festival, or the violent mobs that fed off the smell of fire and the sound of breaking glass. More often than not, I would end my visits to Rickson's by helping one of his kids with a school paper, dancing in the living room with his daughter Kauan, or rewriting PR copy for his then-wife, Kim.

While Rickson taught me about base, connection, and leverage, I taught him about Carl von Clausewitz, the Schlieffen Plan, the War on Terror, and the Khmer Rouge. What has made our friendship unique is that we have always given each other our unfiltered opinions, but always, through life's triumphs, tragedies, reversals of fortunes, bestsellers, and lawsuits, stood shoulder-to-shoulder. "You are the only person I know who can call up my dad some two days before you are in town (if that)," wrote his daughter Kaulin, on the eve of her wedding in 1999, "and get him to put on his rusty old Gi, clean out the garage, and preach his life's philosophy."

Initially, *Comfort in Darkness* was supposed to be a lifestyle guide, a victory lap after the success of our bestseller, *Breathe: A Life in Flow.* This book, however, took a much more serious turn in 2021. During a class he was teaching my son, his cousin Jean Jacques Machado, martial arts legend Chris Haueter, and me, we all noticed an unmistakable tremor in Rickson's right hand. If nothing else, my relationship with Rickson has always been direct and honest, so I asked him about his shaking hand, and he told me that he had been diagnosed with Parkinson's disease.

Unlike *Breathe, Comfort in Darkness* is much more of a collaboration than a ghostwrite. To understand Parkinson's, I was forced to learn the biology and chemistry that I failed in school. My academic colleagues brought Rickson and me up to speed on the science of breathing, the physics of leverage, autophagy, neurotransmitters, synapses, dopamine, and many other aspects of the disease. Sometimes I knew more than Rickson did; other times he refuted my academic understanding with his lived experience. As always, it was an intellectually honest give-and-take whose primary objective was to chart the best course forward to fight this debilitating disease.

Over the past two years, Rickson has shown me his faith in Invisible Jiu Jitsu, the depth of his commitment to it, and how he is drawing on it to fight Parkinson's. Nothing, however, has impressed me more than the classes he holds at his small, immaculate, private Jiu Jitsu studio in Los Angeles. When Rickson puts on his kimono, ties his worn coral belt around his waist, and bows to the photograph of his father on the wall, he also puts his pain on the shelf for the next two hours. During these extremely intense sessions, his students' knowledge of base, connection, leverage, weight distribution, and timing—the building blocks of Invisible Jiu Jitsu—are tested.

No matter the color of their belts, every student fails in different ways. After their collective failures are examined, the real class begins as students feel and test their understanding of Jiu Jitsu's larger concepts. There are no matches, nobody is tapping, and the atmosphere is more Socratic than martial. The lessons are stern and earnest; the lion in winter does not mince words or suffer fools. Afterward, Rickson limps off the mat and his sense of contentment and satisfaction is palpable because Jiu Jitsu's Odysseus is always in Ithaca when he is on the mat.

Comparing the vast majority of Jiu Jitsu teachers to Rickson Gracie is like comparing a nail-gun-wielding tract house carpenter to the master Japanese Miyadaiku woodworkers who built the Temple of Horyu-ji. It took me many years to realize that more than the ability to perform armbars, chokes, and sweeps, what Rickson Gracie gave me was the confidence to fight for what I believe is right, speak truth to power no matter the consequences, protect those who do not have the power to protect themselves, and stay calm and improvise when plans A, B, and C fail. This, in short, is "Invisible Jiu Jitsu" and I will carry it with me until the day I die.

"INVISIBLE JIU JITSU"

BY RICKSON GRACIE

LOVE US OR HATE US, FROM MY FATHER, HÉLIO, TO MY UNCLES CARLOS AND George; to my brothers Rolls, Relson, Rorion, Royler, and Royce; to my cousins Carlson, Robson, Rilion, Renzo, Ralph, Jean Jacques, and Rigan; to my sons Kron and Rockson; to my nephews Roger, Neiman, and Kayron; and to my niece Kyra; no family in the modern history of martial arts has produced more game fighters than ours. This should come as no surprise. Our Scottish ancestors fought off Roman, Viking, and British invaders, and when there was no one else to fight, they fought each other.

Scottish clans were usually commanded by their best warriors. These men led from the front and by example. In the 1300s, a feud between two clans grew so bloody that the king of Scotland ordered their leaders to select their thirty best men and settle their differences in front of him in a battle to the death (Battle of the North Inch).

Even though my ancestors migrated from our ancestral home of Dumfries, Scotland, to the Americas in the eighteenth and nineteenth centuries, they kept these martial traditions alive. During America's Civil War, my relative, Archibald Gracie III, had a horse shot out from under him, then got shot in the arm, and was finally killed by a shell during the Siege of Petersburg in 1864. "In the hottest portion of the field, where his men were falling the thickest and the missiles of death were shrieking for victims," wrote the officers who served under him in their eulogy, "he was there joining in the carnage, dealing heavy blows upon his adversary and encouraging his brave Alabama boys forward." If nothing else—win, lose, draw, or die—the will to fight is in the Gracie blood.

I'm no longer a pro fighter and only a fraction of what I once was, but my invisible power transcends my physicality and will always be a part of me. As age, injuries, and illness have caught up with me, I now realize that Jiu Jitsu is about much more than fighting; it is a metaphor for life. Today, I am most interested in teaching the basic principles of Jiu Jitsu to regular people so they can add strategy, tactics, timing, leverage, acceptance, and hope to their lives.

My uncle Carlos and father, Hélio Gracie, created Gracie Jiu Jitsu to be a system of human empowerment through self-defense. The original curriculum was composed of forty private self-defense classes that focused on preparing students physically and mentally to defend themselves in a real fight. As important as the techniques was the confidence or "Invisible Jiu Jitsu" that they gained in the process.

My father and uncle were passionate, driven, and eccentric men. Carlos usually woke before dawn to meditate under the first rays of the rising sun. He believed that he had extrasensory perception (ESP) and spent most of his time thinking about biorhythms, reincarnation, nutrition, digestion, and food combining. My uncle adhered to Hippocrates's maxim "let food be thy medicine and let thy medicine be food." He spent much of his life designing a diet and lifestyle that generations of Gracie fighters have followed and still follow to this day.

Carlos was a zealous advocate of Jiu Jitsu because he believed that it had transformed his life for the better. Around 1917, he and my grandfather Gastão Gracie watched a five-foot, four-inch, 145-pound Japanese fighter named Mitsuyo Maeda, who fought under the stage name of Count Combat (*Conde Koma* in Portuguese), use technique, strategy, and intelligence during a Jiu Jitsu demonstration in Belém, Brazil. After the Japanese fighter and his family later settled in Belém, he began to teach my uncle and a handful of others his modified style of Jiu Jitsu.

Maeda was one of Jigoro Kano's (Judo's founding father) best students and left his school, the Kodokan, in 1904

to travel to America. After a short stint teaching Jiu Jitsu, he became a prizefighter and never returned to Japan. Instead, Maeda fought wrestlers, brawlers, boxers, judokas, and armed *capoeiristas* and defeated them all during a martial arts odyssey that took him from America to Europe, Cuba, Mexico, and South America. By the time Maeda finally settled in Brazil and began teaching, he was a very accomplished fighter who had transformed Jiu Jitsu into a practical martial art that my uncle, and especially my father, further modified.

Because Hélio was the smallest of the Gracie brothers and weighed only 140 pounds, he did not have the option of using power and strength. Instead, he had to rely on precise technique, perfect timing, and strategic patience. He could not impose his will on his opponents. Instead, he had to wait for them to make a mistake, then capitalize on it. Sometimes it took less than a minute; other times it took hours. Although Maeda gave my family a very strong foundation in Jiu Jitsu, it was my dad who transformed it from a martial art for combat into a martial art for survival that enabled the weak to defeat the strong.

Hélio Gracie was our clan chief. Like our Scottish forefathers, he earned this title with blood, sweat, and tears. Between 1932 and 1967, my dad fought numerous formal and informal bouts and challenge matches against wrestlers, *capoeiristas*, and some of Japan's greatest judokas. He was not just brave; he was also resourceful, creative, and adaptive. Hélio was a martial arts version of the Viet Cong.

At the age of forty-four, my dad came out of retirement to fight a former student who was sixteen years younger and fifty pounds heavier. After fighting for almost four hours, he got knocked unconscious by a kick to the head. Even though he lost, Hélio was proud that he did not quit. From as young an age as I can remember, I was taught that there was no shame in losing, but there was great shame in quitting or not fighting.

By the time I was born in 1959, Hélio Gracie was one of Brazil's best-known fighters. Even as a small boy, my world was shaped by my family's warrior ethos. While other children were learning how to crawl, walk, and run, Gracie children learned Jiu Jitsu.

Both my dad and uncle were polygamists, and between the two of them, they sired thirty children with eight different women. Twenty-one of those children were boys, so there was a great deal of competition within my immediate family. Most weekends all the Gracies gathered at our twenty-one-bedroom *casa-grande* in the mountains behind Rio. There we played soccer, rode horses, and enjoyed family meals prepared by a large staff.

Everything was fun and lighthearted, until my dad laid the big canvas tarp down on the lawn and gathered all my cousins and brothers to practice Jiu Jitsu. When Hélio Gracie stepped on the mat, he was a martial arts master and a point of reference for all of us. My dad did not drink or smoke. He followed a strict diet, and held to a rigid code of conduct. It did not matter if it was fighting for hours, taming a wild horse, or cleaning a toilet, he never asked you to do anything that he was not prepared to do himself.

My dad and uncle truly believed that they were creating a clan of warriors, and our comfort and feelings were never considerations. My brothers, cousins, and I all paid our dues on the mat. Not only was there pain and suffering, but the competition was always fierce, and my dad encouraged it. Hélio pitted us against one another in order to test us and see who was the best. Some of my brothers and cousins rose to this challenge, while others collapsed under the weight of it.

Carlos and Hélio were a united front. From the food we ate, the shoes we wore, the way we trained, even the days we fought, they discussed everything. Whenever there was a question, Hélio would have

a quick conversation with Carlos and then come back to us with their decision.

As a Gracie, I knew that I was created to be a warrior and didn't just want to be a fighter; I wanted to be a champion. My earliest childhood dream was to follow in my father's footsteps and carry our family flag into battle. At a very young age, my dad recognized how good I was at Jiu Jitsu and pushed me to become the greatest Gracie fighter of all time. I never resented or resisted this; in fact, quite the opposite. I wanted to prove to my dad that his faith was not misplaced.

I entered my first Jiu Jitsu competition at the age of six. Because they did not have a category for my age group, my dad entered me into the older kids' division. Although I lost, I didn't feel bad because Hélio was proud of me for stepping up and competing. All I felt was unconditional love and support. As I grew up and began decisively defeating my peers, my dad was never excited because he expected me to win.

After my cousin Carlson retired from fighting and opened his own school, my older brother Rolls Gracie became our leader and family champion. For most of the 1970s, none of my brothers or cousins could touch him on the mat and he was at the very top of the Gracie Jiu Jitsu pyramid. A wonderful man who was full of passion and intellectual curiosity, Rolls was not just my idol; he was also my mentor, instructor, and training partner.

The better I got, the harder Rolls pushed me. Training with him was basically fighting, and through this, I learned how to survive long periods of agony, wait for my opponent to make a fatal mistake, then finish him with brutal efficiency. By sixteen, my Jiu Jitsu was becoming more and more like physical chess. I tried to stay many moves ahead of my opponents, lead them into traps, then ambush and checkmate them. In addition to the physicality that I was born with, I also learned to use my intelligence and powers of observation to spot and seize opportunities. I never knew exactly what someone was going to do, but I didn't need to. Once our engagement began, I used pressure, pain, and discomfort to force an error, then take my kill shot.

By the time I was a seventeen-year-old brown belt, I was catching up to Rolls. When I finally beat him at our father's ranch, I felt bad and did not tell anyone. Even though I was now getting better than him, I still saw myself as the Gracie family's number two man, there to back Rolls up. Part of this had to do with the fact that he was such an inspiring leader. Because he was my uncle's illegitimate son, my father raised him with us, and he unified our fractious family. Rolls led with love and accepted you for who you were, not who he wanted you to be.

When I fought my first professional fight in 1980, I was overconfident and learned a harsh, life-changing lesson about the difference between a professional *vale tudo* bout and competitive Jiu Jitsu. Within seconds of the opening bell, my opponent, a big, scary, seasoned pro fighter, dragged me into deep, uncharted waters and made me fight for my life. Everything had been theoretical up to that point, but in less than twenty minutes, I learned sometimes you don't break physically, you break spiritually.

Afterward, I realized that if I was to become the greatest Gracie, I could not depend on others and needed to be totally self-sufficient. The person who taught me how to do this was a former student of my dad named Orlando Cani, who invented a physical practice that he would eventually call *Biogynastica*. Orlando combined dynamic movement with breathing to get practitioners to use their senses and instincts instead of just their brains and bodies. He taught me how to use different breathing techniques to manage the body's natural reactions to the different emotional states you might experience during a fight: fear, panic, exhaustion, and nervous excitement. With the exceptions of my dad and brother Rolls, Orlando Cani was the most important teacher of my life. He taught me how to see fighting through a more mental and spiritual lens.

I was crushed when my brother Rolls died in a hang-gliding accident in 1982 at the age of thirty-one. He left behind two young sons and a heartbroken widow, and my family was never the same. My brother Royler put it best: "There is an era before and another one after Rolls." With our chief gone, it was up to me to pick up his sword and lead the next generation of Gracies. For almost three decades, I did this with all of my heart. I took on all challengers in the ring, on the mat, and in the street. Although I fulfilled my dream of becoming the greatest Gracie, there was one thing that toughness, stoicism, and grace under pressure could not prepare me for: the death of my oldest son, Rockson, in 2000. My beloved firstborn had spent his entire life flying too close to the sun, and when he finally fell to earth, I could not catch him. I still bear the pain of this loss and will for the rest of my life.

For almost three years, I fell into a deep hole of depression and when I hit bottom, I stayed there, and had to decide whether I wanted to live or die. During my years of grieving and depression, I searched for reasons to be happy again. Although I eventually found them in my children and Jiu Jitsu, I was no longer the same person.

Not only had I lost a part of myself, but my shell of immortality and invincibility had been shattered forever. After my son's departure, I no longer cared about fame, wealth, or glory. All of them had lost their luster. Losing Rockson not only humbled me; it also endowed me with more empathy and compassion, especially for the weak and the fellow wounded. Today, these are the people that I am most interested in teaching, and I will spend the rest of my life helping people learn how to tap into their invisible power.

Recently, I have had to summon Jiu Jitsu's invisible power for the most important fight of my life. In 2021, my right hand began to shake uncontrollably. When I went to my family doctor to find out why, he referred me to a neurologist who conducted physical tests and scanned my brain. When he returned with my test results, the doctor said matter-of-factly, "Your test for Parkinson's disease was confirmed."

In life and in Jiu Jitsu, sometimes you are the hammer and other times you are the nail. When you are faced with unexpected challenges, you can either quit and submit without a fight, or you can take a deep breath and engage. While I might not be able to reverse the effects of Parkinson's disease, I will never cede an inch of ground to it without a fight. Like my father taught me, you can't defeat a person who never gives up.

I will die when I die, but it will be on my feet and not on my knees. Until that day, I will live every day with joy, patience, love, and hope. Life is a long journey on a twisting road, and nobody knows what lies around the next bend or over the next hill. If this disease is the price for my success, my ironic karma, then so be it. I will die a happy man, because I have tasted glory and had the privilege of teaching people from all walks of life how to apply the basic principles of Jiu Jitsu to their lives.

I have great faith and confidence in my Praetorian Guard. I rest assured that the select few who have met my highest standards and to whom I have awarded black belts will also carry on my family's traditions long after I am gone. The martial art of Gracie Jiu Jitsu is safe in their hands. One of them is Peter Maguire, the coauthor of *Breathe* and this book, who has been my student and friend for the past thirty years. Just as I have taught him Jiu Jitsu, he has taught me about history, philosophy, international politics, and surfing. More recently, he and his academic colleagues helped me learn about things I understood physically, but not intellectually: the physics of leverage, the science of breathing, the workings of the body's psychomotor system, and the neurotransmitter dopamine. This knowledge has helped me better strategize and visualize my final fight against Parkinson's disease.

God can take my life, but not my will. I hope to be remembered one day as a martial artist who represented Jiu Jitsu with honor, personal rectitude, and respect. Invisible Jiu Jitsu is not meant to turn average people into fighters overnight. Instead, I want to teach average people the trinity and litany of Jiu Jitsu so that they too can tap into their invisible power.

COMFORT IN DARKNESS

chapter 1

KENSHO

OVER THE PAST DECADE, I HAVE GROWN MORE INTERESTED IN TEACHING JIU JITSU to people who are not athletes or fighters because they are the ones who need it most. However, they are also the most difficult to reach because they don't like the physical debate of Jiu Jitsu. In fact, some people have built their entire lives around avoiding any form of conflict.

Restoring the confidence of a bullied child, an abused wife, or a rape victim can only be done with love and compassion. If you have an open heart, you can put yourself in the shoes of the person you are trying to help. Every time I try to help someone, I first have to use my heart to make a connection.

Many years ago, a chauffeur-driven limousine pulled up to my academy in Rio. A well-dressed man stepped out of it, followed by his seven- or eight-year-old son. I noticed that the father was big, strong, and confident, but his son wore thick glasses, and was socially awkward.

"Mr. Gracie, I brought my kid so you can teach him how to defend himself. I'm losing hope!" the man said by way of introduction.

"He gets bullied every day at school and won't stand up for himself!" What the man said next took my breath away. "My kid is a pussy! I'm not sure if he's a boy or a girl!" I immediately interrupted him: "Wait a minute, sir! I'm looking at your son, and he looks like a champion! In fact, he looks very strong."

How could a father do this to a little boy whose life was only just beginning? It made me sad and angry. I immediately recognized that the problem was not the little boy. It was his father's lack of emotional intelligence and insecure state of mind that was the problem. Whether he meant to or not, he was killing his son's spirit. I made it my mission to restore the little boy's hope. In a case like this, I use Jiu Jitsu to repair and reestablish a person's self-confidence and self-worth.

Teaching students like these has always given me the most satisfaction. "How you doing, Chief?" I said, then extended my hand. When the boy grabbed it, I winced and said, "Ouch! Easy there, champ! Don't break it!" Next, I turned to his father and said, "I told you he was strong." Then I paused and stared into the man's eyes with deadly seriousness and said, "Today you can watch his first class, but I don't want to see you here again! From now on, just have your chauffeur drop him off." The boy peeked up at me for the first time, studied me, then gave me a sly grin.

I walked the little boy onto the mat, adjusted his body so he had a good base, pushed him, and he successfully resisted. "Who said this kid is weak? He is strong!" I yelled loud enough for everyone in the academy to hear. "I can't move him!" By the end of the first class, the boy was proud of his base and the fact that I acknowledged his strength in front of his father. Still, he was so beaten down that he seemed almost afraid to smile.

The boy returned the next week alone and his real lessons began. Of course, I taught him the basics of Jiu Jitsu, but I also played the bad guy, the bully who bothered him at school. "Give me your lunch money!" I'd say, then lunge for his throat. "No!" he'd shout and then use Jiu Jitsu to defend himself against my attacks. Soon, this became his favorite part of class and as he gained confidence, I turned the heat up on him.

"You're ugly!"

"You're uglier!"

"You're weak!"

"You're weaker!"

Very quickly, the little boy got comfortable with my aggression and reacted instinctively to it. I had awakened something inside of him and watched his confidence grow with each lesson.

A few months later, the boy's father showed up at my academy unannounced. "Mr. Gracie, I can't thank you enough," he said. "The school called me today and told me that my son beat up the kid who was bullying him. This is the happiest day of my life. You have changed my son forever!" I thanked the man for his compliment, but also told him never to ridicule his son again.

More than just a great day on the job, this experience awakened me to the transformative powers of Jiu Jitsu. I did not just teach that child martial arts, I gave him confidence that empowered him. Muhammad Ali once said, "It's a lack of faith that makes people afraid of meeting challenges," and I believe this.

A few years ago, a Jungian psychiatrist asked me to teach a class to some of his more troubled patients. None of them were fighters or even athletes. Instead, they were regular people trying to overcome severe traumas that continued to impact their lives. The first man had been mentally abused by his mother his entire life. When I met him, I could feel his anger and tension and see it on his severely drawn face. The psychiatrist asked the Angry Man to describe the way his mother treated him, and he grew even more tense. Because it was obvious to me that he was still her psychological prisoner, I decided to use Jiu Jitsu as a metaphor that would allow the patient to "escape" her suffocating embrace.

First, I had the Angry Man get on the ground, then I put him in a headlock and told him that if he wanted to escape, he had to listen to me and do exactly what I said. Initially, he used all of his strength and tried to muscle his way out of the hold. After that failed, he got desperate, struggled, then got mad, and began to shout.

"Let me go! I don't want to play this anymore!"

"No," I replied calmly.

"LET ME GO!" he shouted louder.

"I'm not going to let you go. If you want to get out of this head-lock, listen carefully, and do what I say."

The Angry Man now realized that I was serious and began to listen. "First, get on your side. Put your chin down to protect your neck and keep breathing." After he did everything that I said, I told him to take a minute to breathe and get calm. "You haven't escaped yet, but you've solved the first and most important problem. You are out of the worst danger," I explained. "Now, you're going to use my power against me. Take your arm, hug my neck, put your shoulder against my face, and drive."

The Angry Man pushed his shoulder into my face, and when he forced me to let go, a real smile came across his face for the first time. "Can I try that again?" he said and wanted to drill this escape over and over. By the end of the class, the pinched look on his face had been replaced by a smile. I asked the psychiatrist to get a mirror. When he came back with one, I handed it to the patient. "Look at yourself," I said. "An hour ago, your face was tight and drawn. Now it is peaceful." He looked at himself and said, "It feels good."

The psychiatrist's second patient was the son of a military officer who dominated and emotionally abused him. More than afraid, he was defeated, sad, and lacked the first student's anger. I had to handle him much more gently. First, I had the Sad Man stand with his back to the wall and then approached him. When I got within an arm's distance, I told him to put his hands on my chest. "Now, when I try to touch your chest," I explained, "I want you to deflect my hands!" I reached for his chest very slowly and showed him how to use his forearms and elbows to deflect my blows. Once the Sad Man realized that he could now prevent me from touching his face, I could feel his confidence surge. After he grew even more comfortable, and physically connected with me, I pushed him a little harder. I told the man to shout "No!" every time I said something that he disagreed with.

"You're a coward!"

"NO!"

"You're weak!"

"NO!"

Not only was the Sad Man now deflecting my strikes, he was also speaking his mind and standing up for himself. Like the first patient, in an hour this man's entire countenance had changed, and his dour expression was replaced by a smile.

More recently, I worked with a Chessmaster who was a true intellectual and had a totally different problem. His confidence level was high, but he was stuck inside his own head. He overthought everything, because his life was guided by what he thought and rarely by what he felt. Psychiatrists, therapy, pills, meditation, yoga, alcohol, Tai Chi—you name it, he had tried it—but none of them had helped him regain his mental equilibrium.

When I first shook the Chessmaster's hand, I looked him in the eye, opened my heart, and asked myself, *What does this man need to feel more secure, decisive, and empowered?*

I decided that my primary objective was to awaken his senses, ground him with physical reality, and first address his insecure state of mind. For me, the sign of a secure state of mind is the ability to

respond spontaneously and reflexively in any situation. Often people freeze like a deer in the headlights in physical or mental conflict and can't devise, much less execute, a strategy. For different mental, physical, or spiritual reasons, they are stuck.

There is a lot of strategy in chess, so I knew that this aspect of Jiu Jitsu would make intellectual sense to this particular student. I was not sure how he would react to the added dimension of physicality because he was out of shape, and his connection with his body was tenuous at best. Once we began to move, I could see and sense that the Chessmaster did not have much faith in his body's ability to do what I was asking of it. Whenever I sensed that his brain was starting to overthink a problem, I stopped whatever we were doing and had him follow me in a simple, basic breathing exercise. A few deep inhalations and powerful exhalations was all that it took to get him back into his body and on track again.

By the end of the first session, the Chessmaster was able to connect with me, but more important, he was able to connect with himself. Instead of being lost in his mind, he was pleasantly lost in the breathing and motion. After just two afternoons together, my new student was using leverage against my power, technique against my speed, breathing to manage his emotions. Not only did he move much more precisely, but his decision-making process was much sharper, and his emotional control had improved. The Chessmaster left LA with much more confidence and faith in his physicality.

The litany of Jiu Jitsu—base, engagement, connection, leverage, and timing—gave the Chessmaster a deeper understanding of himself and a new set of problem-solving tools, whether the problems were physical, mental, or emotional. When we first met, he was running on one cylinder. Forty-eight hours later, he was running on four. Two years later, the Chessmaster still takes a Jiu Jitsu class once a week. Although he only takes private lessons and might never get his blue belt, this is enough for him. I respect him for continuing to step onto the mat.

By choreographing physical dramas and forcing people to solve the problems that I pose, I am able to make them feel and experience the unresolved conflicts and suppressed emotions that trouble and limit them. The same tools they use to solve these physical problems, they can use in their personal lives. While it is impossible to fix all the traumas of a person's past, I can at least give people hope and the strategies necessary to move beyond them.

What is missing from most of the mental health treatments in the West today—whether they involve psychiatrists, psychologists, or counselors—is a relationship with the physical self. This is a much deeper form of analysis than just intellectually recognizing a problem and then talking about it. If I can make a nervous person feel more relaxed than they've ever felt before, I'm changing them from within in a way that a therapist or a pill cannot.

As I have aged, the way I see myself as a teacher has changed and this has broadened my Jiu Jitsu horizons. This has inspired me to create a simpler curriculum for average people who have no interest in colored belts, cauliflower ears, and physical conflict. Even if you are not a fighter, if your mind and body are synchronized, you can make better, more confident choices in life.

chapter 2

THE PROTOCOLS OF INVISIBLE JIU JITSU

LITERALLY SPEAKING, "INVISIBLE JIU JITSU" REFERS TO THE TECHNICAL ASPECTS of the martial art that are not visible to the naked eye because they are too subtle to see. For example, if you took a picture of me on top of an opponent, it would look no different than a picture of another high-level Jiu Jitsu black belt on top of a person. However, the person underneath me would feel the difference, because I use angles and leverage to distribute my weight in ways that create a type of pressure that must be felt to be understood. Figuratively speaking, "Invisible Jiu Jitsu" describes the confidence that the practice of Jiu Jitsu instills in many of its practitioners. One of the earliest Gracie Jiu Jitsu ads proclaimed, "The self-confidence and peace of mind acquired through learning Jiu Jitsu will help solve the problem of human insecurity."

Today, I am adamant that any student I teach, no matter the color of their belt, learns my trinity and litany of Jiu Jitsu, so I will

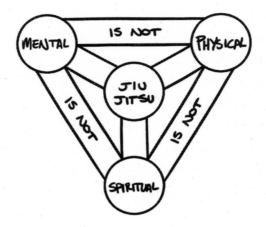

ask the same of the readers of this book. Part encyclopedia and part sacred text, this knowledge was handed down to me by my family. Out of necessity, I also added my own chapters to this book.

Jiu Jitsu is composed of three interconnected, complementary, equally important elements—the mental, the physical, and the spiritual. At the center of this ever-changing trinity lies Jiu Jitsu. The mental is ruled by the rational mind that deciphers and responds to empirical information. If your opponent turns his back, you choke them. If weight is distributed unevenly, you sweep them. The physical is composed of the tasks we tell our bodies to perform: passing the guard, maintaining mount, or executing a throw. The spiritual is the realm of the things we cannot see, but can sense—panic, endurance, acceptance, and hope. After my first pro fight, I realized that if my performance relied too heavily on any one of these elements, I would be imbalanced and never realize my full potential as a fighter.

Each element of Jiu Jitsu's litany—base, engagement, connection, leverage, and timing—has two definitions: a literal one for the mat, and a more figurative or metaphorical one for life. Without an understanding of the trinity and the litany, you can learn all the technical moves (chokes, armlocks, sweeps, etc.), and still have a very shallow understanding of the martial art of Jiu Jitsu. One can mask these deficiencies with speed, strength, and power, but over time, speed, strength, and power fade.

Base is the most primary concept in the Jiu Jitsu litany. It is a state of physical and mental balance that I constantly seek to maintain in Jiu Jitsu and life. Whether you are standing or on the ground, your base represents your physical equilibrium. If you don't have a solid base, you are like a tree without roots. This concept is not exclusive to Gracie Jiu Jitsu. The Japanese martial arts use the word *hara* to describe the center of one's being. The samurai believed that one needs to be "centered" to find order in the chaos and confusion of battle.

To have a solid base, a Jiu Jitsu practitioner must also have the ability to distribute and redistribute their weight spontaneously and unconsciously, without over- or under committing. For example, if someone tries to push me, I'll shift my weight to the balls of my feet. If someone tries to pull me, I'll sit back and sink my weight into my heels. While you cannot see these adjustments, my opponent and I can both feel them.

If my opponent moves just a few inches, I must adapt and adjust my base, like a boat changing its course due to a shift in the wind. Sometimes this only requires me to move my hips a few inches; other times I must move my entire body. This sounds simple enough, but base is difficult to maintain because it is constantly changing. After you have lost your base, it is sometimes difficult to regain it. Now mental and spiritual tools like acceptance and humility become as important as your physical tools. It does not matter if you are in a Jiu Jitsu match, or a lawyer in a trial, the principle is the same.

The sooner you let go of what you are losing, the sooner you can regain your base. Say I am on top of someone and isolating their arm for an armlock. Instead of defending their arm, my opponent grabs my head, squeezes it with all their might, and refuses to let go. While the headlock might be uncomfortable, it will not protect them from the armlock. Instead of accepting the fact that they must release my head to defend their arm, they cling to the head and the illusion of success because they lack the humility to accept that their situation is going from bad to worse. This is no different from a defense lawyer whose client is arrested at the scene of a murder with the murder weapon in hand. If the lawyer clings to the illusion of his client's innocence, he might send his client to death row.

When I ask a student to close their eyes and then test their base, the student immediately feels where they are solid and where they are unstable, wobbly, and weak. Once a student can feel their base, they can begin to turn off their conscious mind and rely more on their intuition and instinct than their brain. Just as a solid base can help you counter a Jiu Jitsu opponent's aggression with leverage and timing instead of just power, it can also be an important tool in your daily life. Psychiatrists use the term "grounded" to describe someone with a strong psychological base who is content with who they are. This quality helps them to analyze information objectively, even when that information does not confirm their preexisting beliefs. In fact, it might even threaten them.

Your psychological base becomes especially important when you are dealing with stress or conflict. If it is weak, you will not be secure enough to analyze information objectively. The inability to see things as they are, and not as you would like them to be, will prevent you from being proactive. Instead of intercepting and engaging small problems before they become big, you will only be able to react and hopefully recover. If you are lucky, your life will become a series of linked recoveries. If you are unlucky, you will eventually zig when you should have zagged and fail catastrophically.

A strong base allows me to be the one who sets the terms of any engagement. I often conduct an experiment to test a student's ability to engage. I walk twenty feet away, then tell them to pretend that I am someone they do not know and to defend themselves.

How they manage the space between us tells me a great deal. As I slowly walk toward them, they should establish a solid base, raise their hands, and prepare to engage me long before I can close the distance between us. When people don't do this, I know that they don't understand a key part of Jiu Jitsu's litany: engagement. This comes as no surprise to me, because many Jiu Jitsu students today spend 90 percent of their time training on the ground and rarely train on their feet. They also don't regularly face punches and kicks, so they don't understand range, where they are vulnerable to strikes and where they are safe. A deep understanding of engagement helps one to recognize the conflicts that they can avoid and those that they cannot.

Imagine that you are walking down an empty street late at night. Instead of looking at your surroundings, you are looking at your phone. Suddenly, a flicker of movement out of the corner of your eye brings you back to your senses. A large, menacing man has stepped out of the shadows and is walking toward you. If you are lucky, you can cross the street, not engage, and avoid the conflict altogether. Sometimes, just this situational awareness can be enough to deter a predatory aggressor. This time, however, it is not.

What if the man also crosses the street and begins to follow you? Even worse, what if he begins screaming like a lunatic and sprints toward you at full speed? Whether you like it or not, you are now engaged. First, you must establish your base, then bring your hands up to defend yourself and deflect punches if necessary. Deflection does not simply mean blocking energy with energy, or force with force. Instead, you not only use your opponent's energy to nullify their attack, but also use angles, leverage, and timing to create the opportunity for a counterattack.

A connection can be physical, mental, or spiritual. In any of these cases, I must be mentally and physically present to connect. If I have a conversation with somebody, from the moment I shake their hand they have my full attention. Things like body language, eye contact or lack thereof, sense of humor, and comfort tell me as much about a person as the words that come out of their mouth.

If an attacker tries to grab me by the throat, as he gets into my range and reaches for me, I will raise my elbows and establish a connection by placing my hands on his chest. As he attempts to get his hands on my neck, I will use my elbow as a lever to lift his elbow. Once my attacker's elbow is in the air, I slip under it, then move to his back, and use leverage to apply a choke. Whatever force you use against me, be it physical, verbal, financial, or intellectual, I will engage, connect, counter, and try to use it against you.

A good connection also enables a person to use leverage instead of just power. When Jiu Jitsu fell into my father's hands, he had to modify it, because his possibilities were limited by his lack of size and strength. Hélio Gracie used leverage to compensate for this. A lever is a simple machine that reduces the amount of effort and force necessary to lift a beam or execute a sweep. For thousands of years, men have used levers to increase their strength. The ancient Egyptians used them to lift 2.5-ton stones to build the pyramids. A child's seesaw is a simple lever with a fulcrum in the middle. If I move that fulcrum closer to the load that I am trying to lift, I can move it with less force.

The human body uses levers all the time. If I pick up a weight to do a bicep curl, my forearm acts as a lever and my elbow joint, the fulcrum. If I try to grab someone with a bent wrist, I might have very strong hands, but without the increased leverage of a straight wrist, I can't utilize my strength. If I straighten my wrist, I immediately feel my power increase.

In Jiu Jitsu, the levers we use can be the body's limbs or even the trunk of the body itself. For example, the lever in a hip throw is my

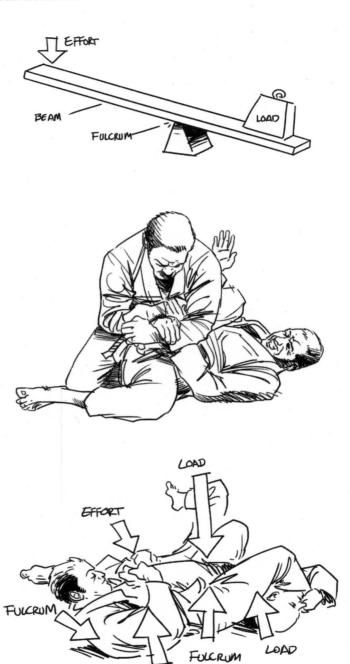

opponent's upper torso. In an armbar, my opponent's arm, from his shoulder joint to his wrist, is the lever.

The farther I get away from the fulcrum of my opponent's elbow, the more leverage I get and the less force I need to straighten his arm to execute the submission. Leverage is also an undeniable fact in daily life and can work either for or against you. Because your boss has the power to fire you, he has leverage over you. If someone owes you a large debt, you have leverage over them. You take out a huge loan to buy a house that you cannot afford, and you have leveraged yourself.

Leverage and timing go hand in hand. If your technique is good, but your timing is bad, you will have a difficult time landing a punch, defending a throw, or sinking a choke. Like the great jazz musician Miles Davis said, "Timing isn't the main thing, it's the only thing." To have good timing, you must also have good perception so you can recognize your opportunities, then act decisively.

Timing is also a constant in our daily lives because it is working either for or against you. Whether you are trying to make an airplane flight, buy a house, or catch a wave, the better your timing, the better your chance of success. Sometimes you can use time to your advantage by taking a strategic pause to consider your options; other times you must press your advantage. It does not matter if you are trying to close a deal before interest rates go up, or finish an exhausted opponent in a Jiu Jitsu match—the principle remains the same.

chapter 3

FEAR

THE TRINITY AND LITANY OF JIU JITSU ALLOW A PERSON TO USE THEIR HUMAN senses to manage the age-old challenges of the human condition like fear and anxiety. These uncomfortable emotions live within all of us. You don't need to be in a Jiu Jitsu tournament, a fight in the Tokyo Dome, or on a battlefield in Ukraine to experience these unpleasant feelings. Scientifically speaking, fear is caused by a rush of adrenaline that is triggered by the brain's fight-or-flight mechanism. As I have said many times, fear is a sign of intelligence that is hardwired into all of us. Anyone who claims to have no fear is either stupid or crazy. Rather than try to stifle this unpleasant emotion, it is better to learn how to manage it.

Anxiety is more a general feeling of dread. This is not a new phenomenon. I am sure the Chinese felt anxious when they saw clouds of dust in the distance and knew that Mongols were approaching on horseback. The Mongols realized this and tied tree branches to the tails of their horses to create more dust and thus more anxiety. This type of anxiety was based on life-or-death, fight-or-flight physical questions.

In the twenty-first century, the sources of anxiety are more complex and multifaceted. Modern aggressors can strike in texts, emails, or social media posts. In America and much of the Western world today, these inevitable human feelings have been reclassified as "diseases," "disorders," or "syndromes." Many go to psychiatrists and treat their anxiety by talking about what they believe to be their problems. Others choose a more temporary pharmacological solution by taking one of the many Food and Drug Administration–approved "anti-anxiety" drugs. While pills can dull or mask these feelings, ultimately they do not address the root cause of the problem. The way the US government treats the veterans of the War on Terror is a good example. Many former soldiers have difficulties transitioning from the zero-sum world of killing or dying to the civilian world where one wrong word or look can cost you your job. Instead of tapping into the veterans' warrior spirit and challenging them with strategies and goals for their new lives, the government sedates them.

I was once so crippled and paralyzed by fear and anxiety that it led to the most transformative experience of my life. I too had to learn how to face, overcome, and manage my anxiety and fear just like everyone else. Like my father, I thought that I was willing to die to prove that Gracie Jiu Jitsu was the most effective martial art on earth.

As Hélio Gracie's son, not only did people expect big things from me, but it also meant that I walked around with a bull's-eye on my back. I suffered so much agony in Jiu Jitsu when I was young. In addition to my brothers and cousins who showed me no mercy on the mat, there were always tough guys in the academy who wanted to put me in my place.

My first experience with irrational fear occurred at my father's academy when I was barely a teenager. A big man caught me in a tight headlock, and as I began to work my escape, his hot, stinky Gi covered my head. Suddenly, I got claustrophobic and was overcome with a fight-or-flight sense of panic. Instead of calmly escaping from the hold like I'd done so many times before, I tapped out in front of my brothers, cousins, and friends.

Ashamed and disgusted with myself, when I got home, I knew that I had to face my demons, so I asked my older brother Rolls to wrap me up in our living room carpet. I told him to leave me inside for ten minutes, no matter how loud I screamed. As the hot, mildewy carpet began to envelop me, I thought for a moment that I might die. Then I started thinking about the beach, a sea breeze, and a cold coconut water. My claustrophobia passed because I found comfort in the darkness, and I lost all track of time. Before I knew it, ten minutes had passed, and my brother was unrolling the carpet. We did this a couple more times over the next few months and it was through this discomfort that I overcame my claustrophobia. As a result, my Jiu Jitsu began to improve by leaps and bounds.

By sixteen, I was traveling to other academies and seeking out discomfort by training with the strongest guys and starting in the worst possible positions. My father brought me and each of my brothers along at our own pace. As good as I was, he was careful to put only the load on my shoulders that I could bear. Sometimes just barely, but he was always there to guide me. After a tough match, Hélio would always talk to me, acknowledge my effort, and offer constructive advice. I never felt hopeless, or like I was disappointing him. Even my cousin Carlson, one of the most competitive people who ever walked the earth, was kind and supportive in his own way. I never felt like I was thrown to the wolves, because I was a wolf. Long before I became our pack's alpha, I drew strength, wisdom, and inspiration from my elders.

My dad promoted me to black belt at eighteen. I had not lost a Jiu Jitsu match in four years and longed to fight my first *vale tudo* match. In my family, getting your black belt is just the beginning. You are now an officer, but only a low-ranking one, like a lieutenant in the army. If you win competitions at the black belt level, you get promoted to captain; if you win a world championship, you become a colonel. A Jiu Jitsu champion does not have the same rank as a *vale tudo* champ, because Jiu Jitsu comes in a box. The rules of engagement are firm and fixed and will be the same, whether you are in Rio, Riyadh, or Redondo Beach. *Vale tudo*, on the other hand, is what separated the Gracie men from the Gracie boys.

When I was growing up, every Jiu Jitsu fighter, even if they never stepped into the ring, used *vale tudo* as their point of reference. All of my dad's students knew how to use the guard to defend themselves from punches, elbows, and headbutts. If a student lost sight of this fact, Hélio did not hesitate to slap them back to the brutal reality of a street fight. If you ever wanted to become a respected general in the Gracie family like my dad, cousin Carlson, or brother Rolls, you had to put it all on the line in real fights and *vale tudo*.

Much more wild, free, and spontaneous than Jiu Jitsu or even MMA, *vale tudo* requires a fighter to draw on the full spectrum of their martial arts abilities. Punches, kicks, headbutts, elbows, and knees add layers and layers of mental, physical, and spiritual complexity, not to mention stress. In Jiu Jitsu, I can sit underneath someone as long as I want. In *vale tudo*, that same position is potentially fatal because of the proximity of my head to my opponent's knees or elbows. The intensity, complexity, and violence, I would learn, can be overwhelming. There is only one way to know if you are prepared to enter this arena, and that is to enter it and find out.

In early 1980, I was in the living room in my dad's Copacabana apartment when the phone rang. My father answered it, and when he said "Leopardo" with a smile, I knew that he was speaking to none other than his former student and adversary, Waldemar "The Black Leopard" Santana. After their almost four-hour fight in 1955, their rift healed, and they became friends once again. After a long career that included fights with my cousin Carlson, Japanese Judo great Kimura, and *vale tudo* pioneers Euclides Pereira and Ivan Gomes,

Santana retired from fighting. Now he was training fighters and promoting fights. He was calling my dad that day to see if he knew of a
worthy opponent for an African Brazilian fighter named Casemiro
Nascimento Martins, who fought under the stage name "King Zulu."
Martins had not lost in years, and Santana was having problems finding anyone willing to fight him.

When I heard my dad say, "He's beaten everyone in northern
Brazil? You can't find anyone willing to fight him?" I began begging
him to match me. "Put me in, Dad!" I said, and Hélio smiled. I could
tell that he was now as excited about this fight as I was. Santana
scoffed at the idea at first because I was still a teenager, but by the
time he hung up the phone, I had a fight with King Zulu.

My first professional *vale tudo* fight was a very high-level debut
in a huge arena in Brasília, the capital of Brazil. Everything that I
had dreamed of since I was a little boy was now within my reach. I
was excited to represent my family and Jiu Jitsu. Reality set in about
a month before the fight when my father and I went to Brasília to
watch King Zulu fight another opponent in the venue where we would
be fighting.

While the crowds at Jiu Jitsu tournaments were passionate and
excitable, the energy at this *vale tudo* event was totally different. Like
the Roman Colosseum, the spectators were there to see blood and
violence. Some of the fights that broke out in the stands were more
exciting than the ones in the ring.

When I first saw King Zulu, not only was his size impressive—
6'4" and 215 pounds—he was also in amazing shape and looked like
he had been sculpted out of granite. The second the bell rang, he ran
across the ring, picked up his opponent, threw him headfirst into the
canvas, and beat him mercilessly. The fight ended after King Zulu
poked his opponent in the eye so hard that he could not continue.

Although I returned to Rio anxious, I was more scared of *feeling*
scared than anything else. Instead of facing these feelings, I masked

RICKSON X REI ZULU

O prestígio dos Grácie — família que introduziu o Jiu-Jitsu no Brasil — está em jogo. Desafiado pelo truculento Rei Zulu, que se orgulha de já haver quebrado vários lutadores, Rickson Gracie levará ao ringue a sua invencibilidade no vale-tudo de amanhã, às 21 horas, no Maracanãzinho.

Um faixa preta que
vai usar a técnica

O antigo segurança
que bate sem pena

them with bravado. As a result, when I went back to Brasília to fight a month later I was spiritually unprepared. On fight night, as I made my way from the locker room to the ring, the spectators looked at me like I was a rat about to be fed to a boa constrictor. I vividly remember sensing more pity from them than hostility. I walked past one lady, and she said, "What the fuck! He's just a kid!" They were expecting a human sacrifice, not a fight.

King Zulu strode confidently past me in the ring. He was so big, muscular, and agile that he reminded me more of a horse than a man. Even though I was very impressed by his size and strength, I was still not intimidated. After all, my most important point of reference as a fighter was my five-foot-seven-inch, 140-pound father. If he could fight men fifty pounds heavier for hours at a time, so could I.

There was only one problem. Mentally I was ready, physically I was ready, but I was missing the spiritual component of the Jiu Jitsu trinity because I was not yet prepared to surrender myself to my fate. My prefight visualizations had been very superficial, mostly of quick, triumphant victories. This would have a deep impact on my performance.

The second the bell rang, King Zulu charged. I held my ground until the last possible second, then threw a knee to his face with all my might and it was right on target. To this day I have never hit anyone harder and was certain that I had knocked my opponent unconscious and that my first *vale tudo* fight was over.

I never could have imagined, much less visualized, what happened next. Like a monster in a horror film that you cannot kill, King Zulu picked himself up from the canvas, spat out blood and bits of teeth, then attacked me again like it never happened. This time, he picked me up and threw me out of the ring headfirst. Just as I was about to hit the concrete, I grabbed the rope, my legs swung underneath me, and I landed on my feet. Thoroughly shaken by the intensity of this conflict, fear began to creep into me and I began to ask myself what I had gotten myself into. Before the fear had time to spread, I was back in the ring and was again fighting for my life.

After a brief scramble, my opponent got me in a brutal headlock. For a second, I felt like my head was going to explode, but I remained calm. After I took the pressure off my neck, I improvised an escape, and took King Zulu's back. Just as I was starting to sink a choke, he escaped, got back to his feet, picked me up, and threw me out of the ring again! For the rest of the round, we traded knees, elbows, kidney kicks, and headbutts. My first pro fight was a blur of nonstop action, an all-out war. Neither of us held anything back, and I gave as good as I got.

It was not until the round ended and I returned to my corner covered in King Zulu's blood that fear spread through me like a fire in dry grass and consumed me. In retrospect, I can see that I wasn't even doing badly, much less losing. Because the action had been so intense, my mind had not had the luxury to run wild.

I was so emotionally overwhelmed that I convinced myself King Zulu was invincible. "Dad, throw in the towel! I have nothing left!" I begged, but he knew better and ignored me. Hélio, the veteran of much longer and bloodier battles, saw the fight very differently. "You're doing fine!" he said calmly. "He's in much worse shape than you are!" "Dad! I'm serious, I can't fight anymore!" I protested, and as we were arguing, my brother Rolls dumped a bucket full of ice and water on my head that shocked me back to my senses. When the bell rang, I stepped to the center of the ring with only two thoughts: kill or die.

When King Zulu and I engaged at the start of round two, he was less aggressive and moving much more slowly. Then it dawned on me. My dad was right! My seemingly invincible opponent was out of gas and trying to rest. This revelation restored my hope and confidence, so I attacked. In no time, I took King Zulu down, got on his back, and choked him until the referee pried me off. Suddenly, the fight was over, and I had won my first *vale tudo* fight by submission.

Although we fought for less than twelve minutes, it was the longest twelve minutes of my life. After the bout, I was relieved, but not happy. For me, the victory was bittersweet, because my dark side, my negativity, almost cost me the fight. I did not sleep that night. Instead, I tossed and turned in my bed and cursed myself for chickening out at the worst possible time.

What became clear to me during that long and sleepless night was that I was my own worst enemy. When it really mattered, not only did I not trust myself, but I also didn't trust my dad, and more importantly, my Jiu Jitsu. Now I had to face the painful reality that my father and brother had saved me from defeat by pushing me way past what I thought my limits were. Had they not been in my corner, I would have quit.

After my fight with King Zulu, I realized that I was only a superficial warrior. Although I was physically and mentally prepared, I was not spiritually prepared to accept any possible outcome in a fight. Even though I thought I believed in myself 100 percent, it was only with my rational mind. I believed in my ability to engage, take him down, and choke him. These, however, are only physical and mental tasks.

It took diving into the deep end and nearly drowning for me to comprehend the gravity of a *vale tudo* fight. It is impossible to understand or prepare for this kind of pressure until you are exposed to the searing heat of it. Everything had been theoretical until King Zulu pushed me to the limits of my ability in ways nobody else ever had. I was fortunate to have experienced warriors like my father and brother to guide me through this darkness and back into the light.

At the start of my career as a pro fighter, I aspired to join my father, cousin Carlson, and brother Rolls in my family's pantheon of great fighters. I religiously followed their different examples, but I realized that I had reached the end of the road that my ancestors had paved. Now I was going to have to break my own trail if I was going to reach my full potential and become the greatest Gracie. After my painful experience in Brasília, I wanted to reinvent myself and grow as a warrior.

chapter 4

FEEL, DON'T THINK

IN THE DAYS AFTER THE FIGHT, I REALIZED THAT MY MIND HAD BETRAYED ME AND now I understood just how important my mindset was if I was to grow as a fighter. After I reevaluated everything that I thought I knew at that point in my life, my first order of business was to confront and defeat the enemy inside my head. Very quickly, thanks to a great teacher, my reinvention became an evolution.

Orlando Cani was a former student of my father, who had developed a methodology and practice to improve human physical performance. He did not believe that the mind alone controlled the body and held a more holistic view that factored a person's emotional, mental, and spiritual states into the equation. After my fight with King Zulu, his approach made perfect sense to me.

Because modern man had been taught to think instead of feel, Orlando believed that we had erected an artificial barrier between the brain and the body. For an athlete to reach their full potential, that wall had to be demolished. The most important tools he used to knock it down were movement routines that combined aspects of yoga, Tai Chi, Kempo, and dance, with different, very conscious, breathing techniques.

Orlando's broad knowledge of athletics impressed me. He didn't just talk about yoga, Judo, *capoeira*, Tai Chi, modern dance, or Jiu Jitsu—he did all of them well. He was once a world-class athlete who competed in swimming and gymnastics in college and studied physical education. After graduation, Cani joined the Brazilian military, became a paratrooper, and began competing in military pentathlon competitions. This multidisciplinary event consists of an 8,000-meter run, different types of shooting (rapid-fire, precision, and long-distance), a 500-meter obstacle course, a 50-meter obstacle swim, and throwing projectiles at targets.

Military pentathlons are held over several days, so it is especially important for competitors to maintain their psychological equilibrium throughout the entire event. To become a top pentathlete, you

have to be able to bounce back from failure quickly. Not every athlete is good at every event. Just because you are a champion swimmer does not mean that you are a champion runner. This led Orlando to the simple, but brilliant, conclusion that what separated great athletes from the greatest athletes was their ability to recover from failure.

After winning his second world military pentathlon championship, Orlando retired from competition, then went on what turned out to be a spiritual journey. First, he traveled to India to study yoga with Shri Yogendra, the father of modern yoga. While in India, Orlando learned of the two-thousand-year-old Indian martial art called Kempo (also known as *Kalarypayat*) and trained at the monasteries where it was still practiced. As much a way of life as a martial art, Kempo practitioners study fighting, healing, yoga, astrology, and philosophy. Unlike Tai Chi, which Cani also studied, this martial art doesn't just attempt to imitate an animal's movements. Instead, practitioners try to feel like that animal, draw on its instincts, then re-create its movements.

After Orlando returned to Brazil, he began to study dance and saw many similarities between it and martial arts. It did not matter if it was fighting, dancing, singing, or acting—the equation was the same, because all these activities required the mind and body to work together under great pressure. To him, they were all unconscious and spontaneous "corporeal expressions."

If an animal is engaged in a difficult physical task, like a pelican gliding inches above a breaking wave, or a bat flying through a pitch-black cave, they are not consciously thinking about what they are doing. Instead, they are acting and reacting unconsciously to the information their senses feed them. These inexplicable forms of unconscious movement led Orlando to rethink athletic performance.

When I went to Orlando Cani's studio for the first time, I noticed that most of the students were dancers, actors, and regular people. Were it not for the ladders on the walls, it would have looked

like a dance or yoga studio. My new teacher greeted me warmly and when he shook my hand and looked me in the eye, I could sense that he was not just a great athlete, he was also an unusually sensitive and perceptive person. Well into his fifties, my teacher had the energy of a man half his age and was in excellent physical condition.

Once the class began, I did my best to mirror my teacher's movements, flow with the energy, and express myself like an animal guided only by instinct. This took my full concentration, and in no time I was exhaling and exploding from the floor like an eagle taking flight, inhaling, dropping to the floor, and slithering on my belly like a snake. I especially loved Biogynastica's changes in tempo and its broken rhythms. No matter what I was doing—soft, hard, slow, or fast—I was always breathing. I got so lost in the movement that I fell into a meditative state, and very quickly, my subconscious mind took control of my brain and body.

After class Orlando came up to me and said, "Rickson, you're too advanced for this class. I respect what you are trying to do and want to help you reach your full potential as a martial artist. I want to teach you privately." Each day we began our training sessions at 2 p.m. and by 2:10, I had left the conscious universe behind.

Over the next few weeks, my teacher choreographed breathing and movement routines designed to develop my creativity as a fighter. Some of the routines drew heavily from monkeys and feline animals, because they use feet and paws, or hands, the same way I use mine in Jiu Jitsu. We imitated the serpentine motions of the snake, because they move by contracting the muscles that run the length of their bodies like I use my arms, legs, and abs to move on the mat. Snakes also constantly redistribute their weight to the areas where their body can get purchase and thrust. Again, my goal was never just to imitate these different animals' movements, but to feel like those animals while I was moving.

Most important, Orlando taught me how to silence the voices of ego, fear, overconfidence, and anger in my mind so these products of my imagination would not cloud my perception. My teacher wanted me to fight in a natural and spontaneous way. To do this, I would need to see things as they really were, not as I hoped or expected them to be.

The psychomotor system controls both the body's brain-based functions (perception, attention, decision-making, and memory) and the body-based physical skills (movement, strength, coordination,

and speed). During my fight with King Zulu, my psychomotor system was so agitated that I could not accurately perceive and decipher information. After my brain had an opportunity to calm down, my psychomotor system regained enough balance to see and sense that King Zulu was exhausted. Once I realized that in the ring, my confidence was restored, and I won the fight quickly.

Orlando believed that the ability to concentrate was something that many athletes, especially fighters, overlooked. By concentration, however, my teacher did not mean thinking and intellectually analyzing your every move during a fight. In fact, he advocated the opposite, because the emotional stress of thinking can trigger an adrenaline dump, which starts a negative chain reaction.

If I am nervous, I get my emotions in check by breathing slower. If I want to pick up my pace, my mind does not tell my body to speed up, I just breathe deeper and faster. By using different breathing techniques, Orlando taught me how to mitigate strong emotions like fear, panic, and claustrophobia and concentrate on what was in front of me, not what was inside of my head.

chapter 5

BREATHE

A HUMAN CAN LIVE FOR WEEKS WITHOUT FOOD, DAYS WITHOUT WATER, BUT CAN'T survive five minutes without air. Orlando called the act of breathing the cycle of life. The human body functions like an internal combustion engine. The oxygen (O_2) we inhale serves as fuel, and the carbon dioxide (CO_2) we exhale is our exhaust. A great athlete who doesn't know how to breathe properly can still run fast and fight well, but they are like a car running on watered-down gasoline.

If I inhale through my nose, the air goes down my windpipe (trachea), then through the two bronchi tubes that deliver it to each lung. Inside the lungs, the bronchi lead into smaller bronchioles then to the alveoli. Like hundreds of millions of clusters of tiny grapes, the alveoli are small, spongy sacs wrapped in blood vessels called capillaries. After the alveoli inflate with air, gas exchanges occur and the deoxygenated red blood cells become oxygenated. During this same gas exchange, CO_2, the waste product, is removed. The freshly oxygenated blood travels from the lungs, through the pulmonary veins, to the left side of the heart (left atria and ventricle) that pumps it to

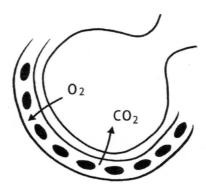

the rest of the body. Simultaneously, the body's exhaust, CO_2, is exhaled from the lungs.

Orlando Cani taught me the difference between a deep breath from my belly and a shallow, panicky breath from my chest (thoracic breathing). When an animal, especially a human, senses that it needs to prepare for action, it begins to take fast, shallow breaths (hyperventilation). Shallow chest breathing is inefficient and is one of the factors that pulls the adrenaline trigger that activates the body's fight-or-flight mechanism. Hyperventilation can also alter the blood's pH level and lead to dizziness and confusion (respiratory alkalosis and hypoperfusion).

Oxygen deprivation is deadly for a fighter because oxygen is your central nervous system's (brain, spinal cord, nerve cells) main source of fuel. When the body stops feeding the brain oxygen (cerebral hypoperfusion), confusion and disorientation follow. If a fighter can't think clearly, they will make bad decisions. If this were not enough, if an athlete does not get sufficient oxygen during heavy exertion, lactic acid will build up in their muscles, and maximum performance becomes impossible.

While inhaling is a reflexive, unconscious action, exhaling requires a conscious contraction of the respiratory muscles (internal intercostals, rectus abdominis, external obliques, and transversus

abdominis). Inhaling can be relaxed, but exhaling to empty the lungs completely requires great effort and you must use your muscles forcibly. When you inhale, the diaphragm, the large, dome-shaped muscle located below the lungs, contracts and flattens. When you exhale, the diaphragm relaxes and returns to its original dome shape. Your thoracic cavity shrinks and this increases the pressure within your lungs and allows air to release passively from your nostrils.

If I am struggling at high intensity for a long period of time, I focus on contracting my diaphragm, which pushes my abdominal wall outward. By flattening my diaphragm, I am enlarging my thoracic cavity. When my rib cage expands and elevates, this creates a vacuum-like effect that will pull fresh, O_2-rich air into the nostrils to maximize my inhalation. It is this O_2-rich air that oxygenates my deoxygenated red blood cells. Then, to get rid of the CO_2, I forcibly contract my internal muscles (intercostals, abdominal muscles, and obliques). This moves the diaphragm up toward the lungs, shrinks the thoracic cavity, then forces air out of the lungs, and ultimately all the unwanted CO_2 from my bloodstream is exhaled.

If my goal is maximum exertion, I'll breathe differently than if I'm trying to recover. Watch any of today's top tennis players and you will see that they exhale at the moment they hit the ball. Not only does this add power to their movement, but this exhalation also helps

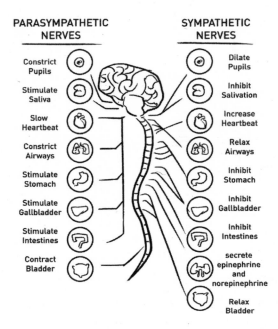

PARASYMPATHETIC NERVES	SYMPATHETIC NERVES
Constrict Pupils	Dilate Pupils
Stimulate Saliva	Inhibit Salivation
Slow Heartbeat	Increase Heartbeat
Constrict Airways	Relax Airways
Stimulate Stomach	Inhibit Stomach
Stimulate Gallbladder	Inhibit Gallbladder
Stimulate Intestines	Inhibit Intestines
Contract Bladder	secrete epinephrine and norepinephrine
	Relax Bladder

lower the amount of tension in their bodies. By using their stomach and diaphragm, they activate their body's parasympathetic nervous system. This nerve network helps calm the body during and after periods of stress. Once it is activated, heart and breathing rates slow, blood pressure drops, and the body begins to relax and recover.

Orlando taught me how to get into a meditative mindset that put me in touch with my primal instincts in a way that transcended my intellectual comprehension. Once I entered that zone, I lived only in the moment without anger, expectation, frustration, or apprehension. When I began to use Orlando's breathing techniques while training Jiu Jitsu, I noticed the effects immediately. I no longer needed to pause to regroup.

By changing my breathing routines, my brain sent a subconscious message to my body to downshift to a lower gear. It was like driving a 4x4 in the sand. When you are losing traction, you can floor it, and if you are lucky, you might power through. However, you might

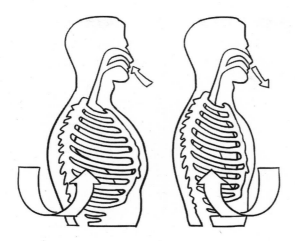

overheat your car or bury your vehicle up to the axles. Conscious breathing let me shift to low range on the fly. This allowed me to push through the friction in a fight without undue stress. Breathing also gave me a sixth-gear overdrive that none of my competitors had, and this made me confident that no opponent could match my pace. I was able to harness all of my energy to focus on either maximizing opportunities or cutting losses. In either case, all of my mental, physical, and spiritual tools were at my disposal.

Some days I came from my classes with Orlando Cani so obsessed with breathing that I tried to make my entire dinner with as little oxygen in my lungs as possible. After I completely emptied my lungs, I cracked the eggs and only allowed myself the tiniest sips of air. It was necessary agony because my objective was to normalize the panic-inducing feeling of being on the verge of unconsciousness. To manage this level of discomfort in a difficult fight, I would need to call on resources that I would not have unless I trained and developed them. By staying on this agonizing edge, my ability to find comfort in any situation increased exponentially.

Thanks to Orlando Cani, I now felt like a pilot sitting in the cockpit of a plane. First, I did my preflight check, then fired up my engine, checked the gauges, throttled up, and took off. Once I was in the air, I unconsciously listened to my engine, kept an eye on my compass, and adjusted my throttle and course without thinking.

I made a deep and profound connection with Orlando Cani. He put into words and motion things that I knew and sensed but could not explain. I had always trained hard, competed at the highest levels, and won. After I trained with Orlando, I immediately noticed that I had a much greater capacity to see and to analyze fine details during a fight. Not only did my perception improve, but so did my reaction time, and this gave me a much broader range of options. Now when I trained, one of the things that I became very conscious of was my opponent's breathing. This gave me another advantage because something as small as a mistimed breath can leave a fighter vulnerable.

The more mental, physical, and spiritual elements of the Jiu Jitsu trinity that I could assemble, the more difficult I would be to defeat. I was grateful to all my Gracie predecessors for adding things to my Jiu Jitsu. In some divine way, I tapped into Hélio's resilience, Carlson's aggression, and the strength of Rolls. By the early 1980s, I had more attributes than any of them.

Curiosity, humility, and gratitude allowed me to reach the next level of performance. To grow, I had to admit what I did not know. Now I could face any problem and find a solution. I was now a much more creative and curious fighter and person. My real test came in 1984 when King Zulu challenged me to a rematch in my hometown. I would soon find out, in the ring, just how much I had improved.

chapter 6

THE UNSENTIMENTAL KILLER

IN THE LOCKER ROOM AT RIO'S MARACANÃ STADIUM BEFORE MY 1984 FIGHT WITH King Zulu, I felt completely different than I had four years earlier in Brasília. This time, before I walked to the ring, I said a prayer and gave thanks for this opportunity to represent my family and Jiu Jitsu. I had no expectations of winning or losing. My only conscious thought was that I was going into battle and was resigned to my fate. I now felt spiritually prepared to sacrifice my life to prove that Gracie Jiu Jitsu was the most complete and effective martial art on earth.

When I was finally standing across from King Zulu, my mind was totally blank and my subconscious was calling the shots. Unlike our first fight, my opponent came out of his corner much more cautiously this time. Of course, he slammed, punched, and headbutted me, but this time, none of it rattled me.

I spent much of the first ten-minute round on my back with the big man inside my guard, trying to punch and headbutt me as I

heel-kicked him in the kidneys. At the end of the round, I returned to my corner with no feelings of fear or panic because I knew that my opponent was running out of gas. When the bell sounded to start the second round, King Zulu started to make strange faces at me and play to the crowd. When he began walking around the ring with his hands at his sides like a wooden soldier, I knew King Zulu was trying to buy time to recover, so I charged across the ring, kneed him in the stomach, and took him to the ground. Less than three minutes into round two, King Zulu made a fatal mistake by grabbing my head and

trying to put me in an improvised Judo scarf hold (*Kesa Gatame*). Not only is this a position that I had escaped from thousands of times, but it is also difficult to maintain with a sweaty opponent who is not wearing a Gi.

Although King Zulu was putting a great deal of pressure on my head and neck, I knew that it would only be temporary. My first objective was not to escape, but to protect my neck, the most vulnerable part of my body. There are times when you are trapped, but instead of using all of your energy trying to escape, you have to accept and endure it until an opportunity to escape presents itself. This is what I mean by finding "comfort in hell." This is more of a mental and spiritual feat than a physical one.

Like a dog distracted by a bone, King Zulu was so focused on squeezing my head that he did not notice when I hooked my leg on the outside of his thigh. The combination of angle and leverage allowed me to back out of his headlock. When my head finally popped free, I was on King Zulu's back, sinking a choke. Seconds later, he tapped out, and the fight was over.

That night in Rio, my ability to align my brain, body, and spirit took me to a new level of human performance. It wasn't that I no longer felt fear, tension, or anxiety—now, thanks to Orlando Cani, I could identify the sources of these feelings and had the tools to manage them. The mental, physical, and spiritual stress that I experienced during our first fight had vanished. The harmony between my mind, body, and spirit allowed me to short-circuit the natural reactions to extreme pressure.

My working relationship with fear gave me a big advantage in the coming years as the pressures on me grew. False confidence is extremely dangerous for a fighter. It usually crumbles during the first hard engagement, and it is replaced by crippling fear. Instead of hiding from it or denying it, I acknowledged my fear and then left it in the locker room.

Panic, claustrophobia, and the fear of defeat were now manageable problems. By accepting death, I truly began to live. As Sun Tzu said, "To win you must know your enemy and know yourself." Now I knew myself, and that I was a calculating strategist and an unsentimental killer.

After my victory over King Zulu in 1984, I wanted to fight the most dangerous opponents I could find. I didn't care if they were two hundred pounds heavier than me, or we were fighting without rules or time limits. I wanted to test myself and prove that I was the greatest Gracie.

Before combat missions, Navy SEAL teams mentally visualize and walk through every step of their potentially fatal missions. They discuss every possible scenario—good, bad, and ugly—and how to deal with each of them. While they hope for the best, they also plan for the worst.

I often did a similar thing and visualized fights with kickboxers, sumo wrestlers, and champion boxers. One fighter I often thought about fighting was Mike Tyson. Although he was younger than me, our careers began to peak at roughly the same time. Tyson's power and technique impressed me, as did his killer instinct. I knew that I certainly couldn't stand in the center of the ring and trade blows with Iron Mike. My biggest fear was the right hand that he used to set up his vicious uppercuts and body shots.

During my daydreams, I imagined myself bridging the lethal gap where I was most vulnerable to Tyson's right hand with a vicious *pissao* kick to his lead knee. My goal was to get him to take his weight off his front foot to defend the kick. Then he would compromise his base and no longer be "set" to throw a lethal punch. This would be my opportunity to take him down or die trying, and it would require total commitment. Even if I ate a punch, I'd have to absorb it and continue to attack. I also entertained more unpleasant thoughts about getting hit by Tyson's spleen-popping body shots and violent combinations. The best that I could hope for in this scenario was to hang on, recover, and recoup enough energy to continue my attack.

Sometimes I would go much deeper in my visualizations and see myself as a lion, hiding above a water hole in the African savanna. Looking down on the zebras, wildebeests, elephants, ostriches, and Cape buffalo, I spot an impala that has strayed from the herd. Before I am conscious of it, I am quietly walking downwind under the cover of the tall grass. As I approach my prey, my mind is calm; my every move is unemotional and 100 percent committed to killing my prey. My desire to kill is primal and nonnegotiable.

I get so close to the impala that I can hear his teeth grinding the grass shoots that he is chewing. When I explode from the cover of the tall grass, my quarry springs high into the air and evades my first attack. As we are landing, I sink my claws into his hindquarters and pounce. The impala's powerful back legs kick me in the chest and I take the blows, then bite down hard on his neck. It does not break, so I clamp my jaws and crush his windpipe. As the animal gasps, struggles, and slowly suffocates, my cubs emerge from the grass. Some tear open the impala's stomach and fight over the entrails, while others pull at the limbs. Soon my cubs are covered in blood and gore, and there is nothing sad or tragic about it because this is an honest,

joyous, even artistic act. The rules of engagement in the animal king-
dom are stern and earnest.

After training with Orlando, when I fought, I felt like my opponents were the impala. They had to deal with the worst Rickson that
you could ever imagine—no mercy, no friendship, no favors, kill or be
killed, quick, clean, and precise—just like the lion. Now I didn't just
want to beat my opponents. I wanted to defeat them physically and
psychologically, without mercy or hesitation.

chapter 7

IMMOVABLE WISDOM

ZEN BUDDHIST MONK TAKUAN SOHO BELIEVED THAT ONCE MARTIAL ARTS TECHniques were learned and perfected, to achieve true mastery, one needed to perform them unconsciously. In a letter to master swordsman Yagyu Munenori, Takuan made an important point about how the human mind can betray you in battle by "being detained" by "any matter at all." He called this "the affliction of the abiding place."

It is not unusual for even an expert marksman to miss his targets in combat, because his mind is suffering from the affliction of the abiding place. Instead of concentrating on the target, he is distracted by "any matter at all." It could be something concrete, like the sound of an approaching helicopter or a bullet whizzing by, but it could also be something more abstract, like the fate of his family, or the fear of death. In any of these cases, his mind is "detained," he loses focus, and he cannot perform at the highest level. To overcome "the affliction of the abiding place," the monk believed that a warrior needed

"immovable wisdom," the ability to act or react unconsciously and instantaneously without thinking.

Takuan Soho's words spoke to me because Jiu Jitsu and fighting had always been 100 percent reflexive and reactive for me. When I connected with an opponent, my brain was relaxed. Sometimes I pressed down on the gas and dared him to match my pace; other times, I patiently waited for my opponent to make a mistake. These decisions were based more on my senses and intuition than my brain.

While I remember parts of different fights, these memories are like snapshots. Once the bell rang and I connected with my opponent, my clearest recollections are blurs of action, like two black mambas fighting. We might go back and forth a few times, but I knew that eventually I would impose my will on my opponent. Sometimes I baited traps, and other times I capitalized on opportunities. In either case, I was not consciously thinking, but flowing and acting without hesitation.

I never thought about winning or losing during a fight. Once an engagement began, I let go of everything and my strategic and tactical decisions were unconscious. When the bell rang, I felt like the volume level in my life was suddenly turned all the way up. Time slowed down and a sense of well-being swept over me. During these fleeting moments, nothing mattered except controlling my body, my emotions, and resolving the matter in front of me with total commitment. This brought me the greatest sense of personal satisfaction and accomplishment in my life.

Nothing else allowed me to express myself and realize my full human and athletic potential like fighting. It is nothing like being on a championship team that plays twenty games each season. If you lose in team sports, there is always someone to blame. When you fight, all of the responsibility is on your shoulders because the outcome depends on you.

More often than not, the greatest human performances are not relaxing or comfortable for the performer. An outnumbered fighter pilot winning a dogfight, a violinist successfully performing a difficult sonata, a rock climber free soloing the vertical face of a mountain, a surfer successfully threading a gigantic tube—in all of these cases, the performers are being pushed to the absolute limits of their ability. All thoughts of money, fame, or glory vanish because they are so absorbed by the activity and the moment.

Neuroscientists are finding more and more evidence that athletes who are preoccupied with a desired outcome, whether it is winning a fight, scoring a goal, or hitting a ball, perform worse than those who are not. They concluded that the faster the planning and decision-making part of the brain (the prefrontal cortex) shuts down, the better the performance. Formula 1 drivers, fencers, and boxers have less than a second to receive and process visual information. Next, they must decide what to tell the part of the brain that sends the electrical impulses to the muscles. Like my decisions in the ring, this action is not analytic and intellectual; it is instinctive, instantaneous, and intuitive.

One of my most important tools, which I use both in and out of the ring, is intuition. For example, I can walk into a martial arts school and immediately feel if the energy is upbeat and positive or dark and negative. It is like reading the ocean. There are days when you go to the beach, the sun is out, and the ocean is flat and inviting. Other days you go to the beach and it's raining, the water is brown, the shore break is smashing onto dry sand, and there are giant waves breaking a mile out to sea. On those days, the ocean is telling you, "If you even get close to me, I'll fuck you up!" Most people can sense and respect this, and have the sense not to walk up to the water's edge.

If I need to evaluate a person, a problem, or a proposition, I pause to allow my heart, where I believe intuition lives, to absorb and evaluate the same information as my brain. After I allow both to review the situation, I draw a conclusion. Many people, especially intellectuals, are wary of their intuition and do not fully utilize their subconscious mind. For them, allowing the heart to overrule the brain is akin to voodoo or witchcraft. In their calculations, there are no human variables like happiness or sadness. It is coldly rational, and often two-dimensional as a result.

My intuition gave me strategic confidence, and this allowed me to be opportunistic. I never had a strict game plan when I entered the ring. Instead, I had a totally open mind and listened, felt, sensed, and searched for any clues that my opponent was unconsciously giving me. My strategy really did not take shape until I engaged with them and received my first set of physical clues. It could be something as simple as his posture, a look in his eyes, or the rhythm of his breathing.

If my opponent was stiff, rigid, and aggressive, I grew soft, pliable, and reactive. If he was soft, or passive, I got aggressive. For example, in one of my professional fights, I noticed that my opponent was distracted by the crowd, so I simply walked across the ring with my hands at my sides like I was strolling through a park. By the time he realized that the fight had started, he was on his way to the ground with me on top of him.

A key element of my strategy was disrupting my opponent's rules of engagement. If he punched, I tried to deflect or intercept his punch, and take his distance away so that he could not throw another punch. Many Jiu Jitsu fighters have taken up boxing and kickboxing to level the MMA playing field. Their improvements in striking, however, erode their ability to use Jiu Jitsu as a martial art, because it changes their ranges, stances, and footwork. I believe that this is a bad trade. It does not make sense to me for Jiu Jitsu fighters, or any grapplers, to stand toe-to-toe and try to trade blows with pro-level boxers or kickboxers. This is like an average Joe trying to beat a pool hustler in a game of eight ball. He might let you win a few times to build your confidence, but sooner or later, you are going to lose and lose badly.

Russian fighter Khabib Nurmagomedov's use of striking to set up takedowns impressed me. Whatever striking Khabib added to his game increased his ability to utilize his grappling. He has a rock-solid foundation in wrestling and sambo. His attacking takedowns were relentless—up, down, clinch, trip, throw, foot, leg, waist—and he never quit. Although he kicked and punched to demonstrate to his opponent that he could fight in any range, strategically speaking, this was smoke and mirrors. Khabib never left the conceptual box of grappling and was disciplined enough to stick to his proven strategy. Sometimes he traded punches to find an opening, but once he took an opponent to the ground, he stayed there. Not only did Khabib finish his fights by submission, but he also maintained his martial art's integrity in the process.

I was never going to try to live an arm's length away from a boxer, because this is his preferred range. Living here makes me uncomfortable, and if I am uncomfortable, I am losing. There are also times, however, when I have to improvise strategically in a counter-intuitive way to solve a momentary problem. For example, when I fought David Levicki, a 6'3", 270-pound striker, he refused to engage. I did not want to box with him, but I had to trade some punches with him to create an opening to take him down. Once I took Levicki to the ground, my problem was solved, and I finished him there.

Typically, I am either going to preserve the gap between us by kicking my opponent in the knees so he can't get close enough to punch, or I am going to bridge that gap and attack with total commitment. "Bridging the gap" and getting into grappling range is always the most dangerous part of a fight for a Jiu Jitsu fighter. This is a no-man's-land that I always passed through with care and total resolve. To make this dangerous passage, precision was more important to me than speed. Even though I tried to move forward steadily, my speed was directly connected to the speed and tempo of my opponent's strikes. To do this, I had to wait calmly and show no cards until he committed to a strike. I saw myself as an octopus. Up until the second an octopus attacks it is perfectly still. However, once a fish swims into range, the octopus attacks with lightning speed.

I always fought with my strong side forward so that I could grab, clinch, trip, throw, punch, and tackle. Once a fight began, my primary strategic objective was to get my opponent on the ground. It did not matter how long this took because I was extremely patient. Sooner or later, my opponent would buckle under the pressure and make a mistake. I didn't care if I was dominating a fight or way ahead on points. I believe strongly, then and now, that when you get your kill shot, you take it and you don't miss because you may not get another.

My goal was always to inflict such a deep and mortal wound that my opponent was dead by the time he realized that he was bleeding. I didn't kill with a hammer, I killed with a samurai sword. I was happy to win quick victories because to me, a win by submission was a win by submission.

My strategic choices were always based on what was happening right in front of me, not what might happen, or what was supposed to happen according to a scouting report or prefight plan. If I couldn't get a choke, I'd take an arm. If I didn't get an arm, I'd go to their back. If I couldn't get their back, I'd mount, fake a neck attack, and take an arm.

Again, the goal of Jiu Jitsu is to use your opponent's energy against him, not stand in the center of the ring and exchange energy. Although wrestling, Judo, and sport Jiu Jitsu all require great toughness and athleticism, they are all sports with well-defined rules that are strictly enforced. As these sports have grown more popular, they have developed around the rules. *Vale tudo* and even MMA are totally different and require a different approach. It is fine to add elements of wrestling, boxing, and kickboxing to Jiu Jitsu, but not at the expense of Jiu Jitsu.

Today, every successful MMA fighter knows a little bit of Jiu Jitsu and everything else. However, just because someone is a gifted grappler does not mean that they can become a gifted striker in a matter of months. Boxing, even kickboxing, leaves a fighter with many vulnerabilities, because their ability to make strategic adjustments is limited by their style. There is no footwork in the martial arts that is more beautiful than boxing. However, it is ineffective outside of a boxing ring because a boxer has to live within an arm's length of their opponent, and is not allowed to fight on the ground.

For many fighters, the inability to improvise strategically is a mental or emotional problem. Over the years I have taught fighters who had talent, athleticism, and discipline, but lacked the confidence to act with Takuan Soho's "immovable wisdom." Instead, they got stuck "in the abiding place." Some could not control their emotions; others simply lacked the killer instinct and could not finish fights.

One student, who was also a friend, let a fight go to the judges instead of taking a risk by attempting a submission and going for the win. In the end, the referee awarded the fight to his opponent, and he lost a bout that he should have won. I said nothing until he began to complain about the judges. At that moment, a yellow flag went up in my mind. While I will never rub anyone's face in their failure, I will not reward, encourage, or help someone rationalize it. I cut him off midsentence and said, "Your biggest mistake was allowing the judges to decide the outcome of the fight."

When I was an active fighter, I could not afford intellectual dishonesty because I had to live in the moment and evaluate every person who came into my life very critically. This meant that I had to be brutally honest, not just about myself, but also about those around me. Were they friend or foe? Were they a fair-weather friend or loyal? This is not an easy way to live.

In the ring, my goal was always the same. I wanted to exploit my opponent's weaknesses, avoid his strengths, and win as quickly and easily as possible. I always tried to see a conflict through the eyes of my adversary. Even if I did not like what I saw, I forced myself to have the courage and intellectual honesty to draw an accurate conclusion. When it came to tactics, how and what I did in a fight, thanks to Orlando, I was no longer burdened by conscious thoughts. By the mid-1980s, when it came to fighting, I had Takuan Soho's "immovable wisdom."

chapter 8

RULES OF ENGAGEMENT

CONFLICT IS AN INEVITABLE PART OF OUR LIVES. IT IS ALWAYS IMPORTANT TO remember that every conflict has its own rules and they can change in the blink of an eye. In a war, each side has official "rules of engagement" that define the circumstances and ways in which soldiers can use force. In the heat of battle, however, these rules can change, because they are dictated by the actions of the individual combatants. If one side tortures prisoners or commits atrocities against civilians, often their adversary will follow suit. Not only have the rules of engagement changed, the conflict has now escalated.

Say two men bump into each other on the street, then exchange harsh words and square off to fight. Suddenly, one of them pulls out a knife and brandishes it in a threatening manner. Not to be outdone, his adversary draws a pistol from his waistband. What was once a fistfight is now escalated into a life-or-death affair because the rules of engagement changed.

In martial arts, there are also rules of engagement. All of my fights in the ring were governed by clearly defined guidelines enforced by a referee. Both times I fought King Zulu, he tried to poke me in the eyes. Although this was a violation of the ground rules, I didn't stop in the middle of the fight and cry to the referee. Instead, I simply accepted the fact that the conflict had escalated and adjusted my actions to reflect this shift.

My street fights and challenge matches were a different matter because the terms were much more fluid and often dictated by my opponent's actions. After I beat King Zulu the second time, I was the man to beat in Brazil, and any fighter who could defeat me would instantly make a name for themselves. In 1988, word reached me that Luta Livre fighter and future UFC champ Marco Ruas wanted to fight.

Luta Livre, or freestyle fighting, is a Brazilian martial art that combines wrestling, Jiu Jitsu, Judo, and striking, and has had a rivalry with Jiu Jitsu and my family for decades. At that time in my life, I did not and could not allow a legitimate challenge to go unanswered. I believed that I was the best fighter in Brazil and had to maintain my reputation by fighting.

After I told my dad that Marco Ruas wanted to fight me, we drove straight to the Luta Livre gym. When we arrived, he and some of their top fighters were training. I first spoke to Ruas and his coach and told them that I had come to fight. Marco said that he wanted to fight, but also wanted time to train and have an official bout. This upset me because I felt like he was more interested in capitalizing on my name than fighting. As I continued to argue with Ruas and others, I heard a voice in the back of the group of Luta Livre fighters say, "I want to fight too." From the second my eyes met Hugo Duarte's, I knew that he was someone who believed he could beat me. At that time, I did not know who he was, but after I left their gym, I quickly learned that he was Luta Livre's number two fighter. Now I took him very seriously because he was a solid opponent who deserved my respect.

I was about to leave for the US and did not have much time, so I proposed we settle our differences at Pepe Beach. On the day of the fight, my brothers, our students, and I assembled at the Gracie Barra school near Pepe Beach. Just before we left to meet Hugo, I told everyone, "It is better that Hugo and I fight than for this to turn into a gang war with people shooting each other. Form a human circle around us and no matter what happens, nobody is to jump in or interfere."

When I first saw Hugo at the beach, I could sense that he was not afraid, but also suspected that he did not have a clear game plan, so I slapped him to draw an emotional reaction. Even though I beat Hugo in a chaotic fight, afterward we jumped in the ocean to wash off the blood, sweat, and sand. As we were leaving the water, Hugo turned to me and said in a very honest way, warrior to warrior, "I'm not happy, I want to fight you again." He was not angry, and the words came from his heart. I immediately knew that there would be a rematch.

A week or so later, a big group of Luta Livre fighters and their supporters invaded my dad's school. A friend rushed to my apartment and told me that Hugo was at my dad's academy demanding a rematch. Still in my underwear, I jumped on the back of his motorcycle, and ten minutes later I was preparing to fight Hugo Duarte on a concrete patio surrounded by Luta Livre fighters and their gangster supporters.

Before the fight, I made it clear to Hugo that if any of them jumped in, this fight would escalate into a war. He gave me his word that this would be a one-on-one fight. Even though he surprised me by showing up unannounced, I didn't feel like Hugo had acted dishonorably. He was a warrior and was not convinced that I could beat him again, and I felt obliged to give him that opportunity. It was only fair.

Hugo was a very different, more purposeful fighter the second time around. He was now the aggressor, the one initiating the fight, so I made a strategic shift. Instead of rushing in to force an entry like I did in our first bout, I sensed that he wanted to knock me out so

HUGO DUARTE x RICKSON GRACIE

I baited him into trying to throw a knockout punch. It was like an old-fashioned duel with flintlock pistols; we each had one shot. Hugo took his by throwing a big punch, and he missed. Then I took him down, mounted, and began hitting him in the face.

Because we were fighting on concrete, every time I hit him, the back of his head hit the ground. He was trapped, taking a lot of punishment, and had no way to escape, so I asked him if he had had enough. When Hugo said yes, I stopped hitting him, and the fight was over. I felt no need to injure my opponent. In fact, I respected Hugo Duarte because he was brave and tough and fought with all his heart.

Afterward, Hugo stood up, shook my hand, and showed me a great deal of respect. He admitted defeat and said that he didn't want to fight me anymore. His words were not only humble and honest, again they were from his heart. Hugo had put everything on the line and come up short. He was not happy, but accepted the result. Even though he lost our fights, he won my respect for his courage, commitment, and willingness to engage. Ours were battles that we could both be proud of because we met on a level playing field and tested ourselves and our skills.

There are other times when brutality can only be countered with brutality. If I see two guys fighting on the street, I might stop to watch, but I won't intervene unless one of them is getting beaten up badly. But if I see two guys attacking a woman, I am going to intervene because they have crossed what to me is an ethical point of no return. In a situation like that, I will act immediately, even if it means getting hurt. While I would prefer to be armed with a gun or a baseball bat, a trash can or two-by-four will do. Ideally, I would like to stop the attack without hurting anyone, but I also must engage with commitment and aggression.

I ran into a situation like this after I fought in Japan in 1994. The Japanese MMA fans thought their pro wrestlers were invincible. My victory in the Japan Open raised an obvious question: How would I fare against one of them? In the fall of 1994, Nobuhiko Takada, Japan's Hulk Hogan, challenged me to fight. I figured this was a publicity stunt designed to get me to fight in the pro wrestling league that he controlled, so I ignored him. As I have said before, I wanted no part of these physical soap operas and no amount of money could make me change my mind. When Takada told the Japanese media that I was afraid to fight him, I issued a press release and said that I would never fight in any professional wrestling promotion, but invited Takada to fight me in the next Japan Open.

I didn't give this drama a second thought until I was awakened by a phone call on the morning of December 7, 1994, the fifty-third anniversary of the Japanese attack on Pearl Harbor. Luis Limão, the head instructor at the Pico Academy, informed me that a Japanese wrestler, his manager, a translator, and members of the press were at my school and they demanded to see me. When I arrived, I saw the reporters assembled by the door, walked inside, and was greeted by retired wrestler, now a pro wrestling official, Shinji "Tiger" Sasazaki. Once again, he invited me to fight in their pro wrestling organization.

After I said no, Sasazaki asked if it was true that I was willing to fight for honor. I replied yes and he asked me if his fighter could come into my school. When I again said yes, Takada's protégé, pro wrestler

Yoji Anjo, one of the bad boys of pro wrestling, marched into my academy. We locked eyes and I could feel his confidence. I immediately knew that he wasn't there just to fight. He wanted to hurt me and make an example out of me for disrespecting Takada. It was a bold gambit.

Anjo showed no emotion and my intuition told me that he was willing to fight me to the death if necessary. This impressed me and forced me to prepare to do the same. More than a *vale tudo* bout, this was more like a showdown between the leaders of two samurai clans. One of us, or more likely both of us, was going to get hurt, and we both accepted it.

Anjo followed me to the center of the mats. I could see and sense that he was blinded by his desire to knock me out and hurt me. I baited him into an exchange of punches and kicks. When I got him in a clinch, even though he was in a bad position, his will and malice never wavered. In fact, he was now even more dangerous, because he was like a cornered animal. Instead of responding to this predicament with fear, he reacted with total viciousness, and stuck his finger in my mouth, then tried to rip it through my cheek.

Now I realized that I would have to break Anjo to stop him. He was never going to quit or submit. After I got his finger out of my mouth and took him down, I moved Anjo to the center of the mats. Then I punched and elbowed him in the face until his eyes were closed and his nose was bloody and broken. I made sure that he was sufficiently marked before I choked him unconscious so that there would be no doubt about who won this one-sided fight.

A few days later, an extremely humble, black-eyed, swollen-faced Yoji Anjo returned to my academy. He offered me gifts, a written apology, and seemed truly defeated. Anjo told me that he respected me and did not want to fight again because he knew in his heart that I could have hurt him much worse. The choice was mine and mine alone. After this meeting I thought that we had settled our differences honorably. The last thing I expected was for him to go back to

Japan and tell lies about our fight. When he returned to Tokyo, Anjo claimed that my students and I had jumped him. Unfortunately for him, I had the only video of the fight. After my representative in Japan called a press conference and played the tape, my reputation with the Japanese grew even larger.

There was only one way to prepare for confrontations like the one I had with Anjo and that was to always be prepared, day or night, 365 days a year. When I was challenged or called out, my only options were acceptance and then action. This was one of the reasons that my daily diet, exercise, and training protocols were so important to me. If I followed them honestly, I would always be ready. After a victory, I never stopped to rest on my laurels and admire myself. Instead, I went back to my academy and trained and taught like it never happened.

chapter 9

INSPIRATION

ALL FIGHTERS INVEST A GREAT DEAL OF TIME IN LEARNING, PRACTICING, AND PER-fecting their techniques. Boxers learn how to throw a jab, a cross, a straight, then practice using them in combinations. Judokas, sumo wrestlers, and wrestlers master pushes, tackles, trips, and throws. In Jiu Jitsu, we drill chokes, armlocks, sweeps, and escapes. The very best fighters, of all styles, use their techniques in ways that reflect their true nature and personality. I learned a great deal by studying other fighters and athletes, and using them as points of reference.

Of course, my father, Hélio Gracie, was my first and greatest inspiration. My dad could be harsh and uncompromising, but without his example as a fighter and dedication as a teacher, Jiu Jitsu would not be what it is today. Anything my dad asked me or anyone else to do, he had done, or was willing to do, himself.

Although Hélio Gracie was a warrior, he was not a traditional warrior and did not define himself by his capacity to conquer and kill. Because he usually fought much larger men, his primary focus was on survival, and this required as much mental strength as physical.

Take the guard position, for example. I doubt the great Jiu Jitsu master Mitsuyo Maeda needed to rely on it. Hélio, on the other hand, developed such a powerful and sophisticated guard because he had no other option.

I think that the fight my father was proudest of was his 1951 bout against one of Japan's Judo greats, Masahiko Kimura. Between 1936 and 1950, Kimura did not lose a single match, and was the only man to win the All-Japan Judo Championship three times in a row. He outweighed my dad by forty pounds, and the second the fight started, he grabbed Hélio's Gi and had him in his control. Like my match with wrestler Mark Schultz, my father's first goal was to minimize the damage of his opponent's brutal takedowns.

At one point during the fight, my father went unconscious, but because he did not tap, Kimura thought that his technique was not working. After he released his hold, Hélio came back to his senses and resumed fighting. Although he threw my father at will, he did not submit my dad until the second round when he caught him in a shoulder lock called a *Gyaku Ude Garami*, what we now call a "Kimura" in his honor.

Because my father spoke so highly of Kimura, he was the first fighter outside my family that I really became interested in. I quickly

learned his success had as much to do with his incredible work ethic as it did his strength, genetics, or natural athleticism. Every day before *randori* (sparring), Kimura did five hundred push-ups, bunny-hopped for a kilometer, then did sets of sit-ups, squats, and headstands. The judoka practiced his leg sweeps against a tree, and his *Osoto Gari* throw was so powerful that he regularly knocked his training partners unconscious.

The night after Kimura won his first All-Japan Judo Championship in 1937, he was back in the dojo and instead of five hundred push-ups, he did a thousand. At the peak of his career, Kimura's daily training regimen supposedly took eight hours to complete. Like many great fighters, he also looked outside of Judo for techniques that he believed would give him an advantage. When Kimura wanted to gain hand strength, he began to study karate with Kyokushin karate master Mas Oyama. He later said that karate's *makiwara* training improved his hand speed and strength, and this gave him an advantage in Judo.

The other Japanese fighter who really inspired me was sumo wrestler Chiyonofuji "Wolf" Mitsugu. The Japanese called Mitsugu "Urufu," or wolf, because of his large eyes, slim face, and aggressive fighting style. He weighed only 260 pounds, which is extremely light for a sumo wrestler. Nonetheless, by the time he retired in 1991, Mitsugu had the most career wins in the history of professional sumo wrestling and even beat the six-hundred-pound Hawaiian, Konishiki.

Sumo is a game of base and position. To be the king of the sumo circle, you must combine strategy and tactics with your personal and physical attributes. Most people don't realize what skilled martial artists the *sumotori* (professional sumo wrestlers) are. Their schedule is among the most grueling in combat sports. They fight in six tournaments a year and each tournament lasts fifteen days, so they fight as many as ninety days a year!

Mitsugu would sometimes have as many as twenty-five consecutive matches in a training session, and before he even turned pro, he had already broken the bones in one of his shoulders many times. He won his first major tournament in 1981 by defeating one of the great Yokozuna (highest ranking in sumo). It was a huge upset and he proved that this was not a fluke by beating the same man again a few months later. Even after he became a superstar, Mitsugu never lost his edge.

What made Chiyonofuji Mitsugu so interesting to me was that he was very nimble and moved more like a boxer than a sumo wrestler. If an opponent exploded at him out of a crouch, he sidestepped at the last moment and sent his opponent sailing out of bounds. Mitsugu had an effective trip that he used in clinches and put much larger men on their backs. What he lacked in size and strength, he made up for with perseverance, agility, and, above all, creativity.

No boxer made a bigger impression on me than Muhammad Ali because he had so many attributes as a fighter. Not only was he incredibly creative, but he had an uncanny sense of distance, not to mention confidence and showmanship. Ali did not move like a heavyweight and masterfully used his "dancing jab" as a range finder to set up his powerful right cross. Many thought the "Ali shuffle," when he moved his feet back and forth and side to side so fast you could barely see them, was just showing off. In fact, this distraction provided cover for both offensive attacks and defensive retreats. He once said that whenever he did the shuffle, his opponent forgot whatever he was planning to do.

It was not until the "Rumble in the Jungle," his 1974 fight in Zaire against George Foreman, that I understood Muhammad Ali's depth as a warrior. Foreman was 40–0, and most people thought that he was much too powerful for Ali. Instead of running, he used his now-famous "rope-a-dope" strategy. To the untrained eye, Ali appeared to be standing against the ropes and letting Foreman whale away at him. In reality, he was blocking and deflecting most of his opponent's punches, then countering with crisp punches. It was like Ali was saying, "Fuck you, George! Your energy has been wasted! Now I'm going to show you what boxing is all about!"

Muhammad Ali was also a great actor in the ring, and this is yet another important aspect of fighting. During the Rumble in the Jungle, Foreman landed a big shot to his jaw that nearly knocked him out. Instead of going down, he held on to his opponent and whispered into his ear, "That's all you got, George?" After the fight, Ali admitted that he was out on his feet twice during the bout, but he never let Foreman know. Before he defeated Foreman physically, he defeated him mentally and spiritually.

What impressed me most about Muhammad Ali was that he had the courage to follow his heart both in and out of the ring. When the US tried to draft him for the Vietnam War, he did not run to Canada and denounce it from safe asylum. Ali walked into the army draft center with all the other young men and when his name was called, he refused to step forward. He bravely asked, "Why . . . go ten thousand miles from home and drop bombs and bullets on brown people in Vietnam while so-called Negro people in Louisville are treated like dogs and denied simple human rights?"

The world heavyweight boxing champ was arrested and convicted for refusing to be drafted. For refusing to go to Vietnam, Muhammad Ali was stripped of his heavyweight title and state boxing commissions refused to license him. The champion was not allowed to fight during the prime years of his fighting career (1967–70). Still, Ali never wavered and his conviction was eventually overturned. Like Ali, I would never have made a good soldier because I could not fight blindly for a government or cause that I did not believe in.

One of the most passionate and emotional fighters I ever watched fight was Mike Tyson. For sheer power and killer instinct, nobody impressed me more. Tyson didn't just want to beat his opponents; he wanted to defeat them psychologically so that they never wanted to step back into the ring with him again. His first-round knockout against Michael Spinks is a good example of this.

Although he boxed during my lifetime, Tyson fought like a boxer from an earlier era, because Cus D'Amato, his coach and father figure, had been coaching boxers since the 1930s. Tyson's references came from older fighters like Joe Louis and Jack Dempsey. His use of angles, timing, and infighting skills was second to none.

Mike Tyson was always very honest about the fact that he fought from a place of insecurity and fear. The boxer came from a broken

home and by the time he was thirteen, Tyson had been arrested more than fifty times. He freely admitted that he was scared every time he got into the ring, but added that he drew power from his fear. Again, fear is in all of us; it's what we do in the face of it that matters. In Tyson's case, he planted his feet, let his hands fly, and dared his opponent to trade power with him.

When fighting or any other sport is your only hope, there is a hunger and drive to succeed that is very difficult to replicate or manufacture. If you've personally experienced hopelessness, hunger, and financial destitution, it can give you a decided advantage. Look at the recent successes of African fighters in the UFC or Brazilians in pro surfing. Not only do they have passion, but they will also die trying to win, because they are the ones feeding their extended families. They know in the backs of their minds that if they don't succeed, they'll be digging ditches or cleaning fish with their fathers and brothers. Fearing that he had grown soft, days before he fought Larry Holmes in 1988, Mike Tyson put on a ski mask and begged for money in the streets of New York. He later said that he wanted to remember what it felt like to be desperate.

Another true warrior I respected for his honesty was boxer Marvin Hagler. Even though he had excellent technique, Hagler always squared up to his opponents. When he stepped to the center of the ring, it was to trade blows. His strategy was always to push the fight to the limit. Very few boxers seek out that level of intensity in a confrontation; in fact, many use technique and strategy to avoid it. Hagler always fought with courage and an open heart.

There is no combat sport, even boxing, that can match the level of intensity of kickboxing. It is even more stressful and brutal than boxing because boxers only have two weapons, but kickboxers have eight. They are allowed to strike with knees and elbows. There is no way to become a kickboxer without conditioning your body to absorb leg kicks, knees to the body, and continue fighting. Of course, the Thai champions of Bangkok's Lumpinee Stadium were the best for their weight, but the Dutch heavyweights, especially Peter Aerts and Ernesto Hoost, were equally impressive. They were true martial

artists who not only fought with great courage and commitment, but also acted honorably in the ring.

Although he never fought professionally or even competitively, Bruce Lee impressed me as a martial artist and teacher. I did not believe that he could do some of the things he did on the screen in real life, but I enjoyed watching him. Surrounded by enemies, but always calm, committed, and resigned to his fate, Lee inspired me.

Bruce Lee came from a very traditional kung fu background and was a student of Ip Man, the legendary kung fu teacher in Hong Kong. After Lee arrived in America, pro wrestler and champion judoka Gene LeBell opened his eyes to the power of grappling on the set of a television show they both worked on. Lee could have pretended that he had never been manhandled by the much larger wrestler. Instead, he began to study grappling with him and incorporated it into his martial art. Lee also became a student of boxing, kickboxing, Judo, and fencing.

In the end, Bruce Lee cherry-picked pieces from different martial arts and then assembled them into his own style, Jeet Kune Do. His view of fighting was very sophisticated, way ahead of its time. Lee broke down a fight into different ranges, then identified the best tools for each range. Like me, he believed in simple, perfectly timed and executed techniques and understood that simple did not necessarily mean easy. Bruce Lee had an open mind, confidence, intellectual curiosity, and the humility to accept new ideas.

Although Pelé was not a fighter, I have to include him as a great inspiration not just to me, but to every Brazilian of my generation. There are very few athletes in sports who are universally considered the best, and Pelé was one of them. I was just a young kid when he was at the top of his game, but I still remember the 1970 World Cup when number 10 led the greatest soccer team in Brazilian history to victory over Italy.

Most players see the ball and whatever is happening in front of them. Pelé saw the entire field; it was like he had eyes in the back of his head. He could improvise better than anyone in soccer and made miracles happen on the field. What I admired most about Pelé was that even though his technical skills were superior to everyone else's, he was a team player who brought out the best in his teammates.

Big-wave surfer Kai Lenny is another nonfighting athlete who has amazed me. He is only thirty-one years old, physically nothing special, but his relationship with the ocean borders on the supernatural. Surfing, windsurfing, hydrofoiling, stand-up paddling, tow-in surfing, he does them all at a world-class level. Lenny surfed Jaws, one of the world's most terrifying waves, at fifteen. In 2017, he rode his hydrofoil between the islands of Molokai and Oahu, thirty-two miles, in less than three hours. By his twenties, he got so far ahead of his competition that he had no peers and had to create his own mental and physical protocols to evolve as a waterman and a human.

What all the fighters and athletes I looked up to had in common, irrespective of their martial art or sport, was that their performances were intensely personal. They were expressions of who they were. When you are exhausted, hurt, and hanging on by a thread, whether you like it or not, your true nature, your true personality, will be revealed.

chapter 10

NEW CHALLENGES

AFTER MY FIGHT WITH KING ZULU, I WANTED TO FIND NEW AND BIGGER CHALlenges outside of Brazil. I traveled to Japan because it is the birthplace of Jiu Jitsu, and home to some of the world's greatest warriors and martial arts traditions. I wanted to meet with fight promoter Antonio Inoki and try to set up a *vale tudo* fight. Best known as the Japanese wrestler who fought Muhammad Ali in 1976 in an odd and early MMA fight, Inoki was one of the pioneers of pro wrestling in Japan and also one of the first MMA promoters.

At that time, Inoki was starting his political career, he would soon be elected to office, and was already a powerful man. The wrestler lived in Brazil during his teen years, and still had a strong connection to the country. I had a letter of introduction and believed that my chances of meeting him were good.

After I arrived in Tokyo, I got little more than an acknowledgment that Inoki had received my letter, and the waiting game began.

At the time, I did not understand how different Japanese society was from my own. Brazilians are passionate people who tend to wear their hearts on their sleeves. The Japanese are much more guarded and harder to read.

Even though Japan is a largely homogeneous society, it is also a stratified one where individuals put the harmony of society above their individual dreams and aspirations. Unlike America, there is no assumption of equality. It is often difficult to get a straight answer to a question, because in the Japanese culture, turning down a request or disagreeing publicly can cause humiliation or "a loss of face" (*mentsu wo ushinau*) that will affect a person's reputation and social standing. For example, a junior executive will never publicly disagree with a senior executive.

Behind the formality and strict rules of decorum in Japan are many layers of unseen activity. I learned this when I made my spiritual pilgrimage to Judo's world headquarters, the Kodokan. Founded in 1882, this school is especially important to me because Jiu Jitsu and Judo's roots are intertwined. Jiu Jitsu was a form of battlefield self-defense that Judo's founder, Jigoro Kano, modified to create a martial art that could be practiced by young and old. To do this, he had to eliminate the more dangerous Jiu Jitsu techniques so that Judo could be practiced with full force and less risk of injury.

The Kodokan always loomed large in my mind because it was part of my family's history. Not only did my father fight Kimura, but Japan's greatest unsung martial artist, my uncle's teacher, Mitsuyo Maeda, was once a champion there as well. When I first walked inside the big, eight-story building, it reminded me of a cross between a church and a military academy. You could feel the respect everyone had for each other, and for the sport of Judo. The instructors and students both had clear missions and were extremely serious about them. The main training hall was very large, immaculately clean, and well organized.

A senior instructor gave me a tour and was very gracious until I mentioned that I was in Japan to speak with Antonio Inoki about a professional fight. Then the expression on his face immediately changed, and he said, "Unfortunately, you can't train here. Judo is an amateur sport, and we don't allow professionals." It was clear that the issue was not up for discussion or debate. After the tour ended, he showed me to the door. I was disappointed but accepted and respected their rules.

Not only did I not get to train at the Kodokan, but Inoki also refused to meet me. Even though this trip now seemed like a waste of time, it gave me my first glimpse of the complexity of Japanese society. This knowledge would serve me in the coming years. Even then, I sensed that something deep lurked behind the fake smiles and ritual politeness. I would soon learn that the Japanese had a deep understanding of every form of conflict. If nothing else, I knew that one day I would return.

Instead of fighting in Japan in 1988, I decided to move my family to America. My father wanted my brothers, my cousins, and me to help my older brother Rorion spread Gracie Jiu Jitsu throughout the United States. Rorion is an excellent teacher and given the success of "Brazilian Jiu Jitsu" and the UFC today, history should remember him as Jiu Jitsu's greatest promoter. Although Rorion had courage and determination and never backed down, he never reached my level as a fighter. Once he got to the US, he faced the challenge of spreading the art by fighting those who doubted its effectiveness.

By the time I arrived in California, the *Gracie in Action* video series that featured me and other family members fighting *vale tudo* and Jiu Jitsu matches had captured the American martial arts world's imagination. This truly was the beginning of a revolution that forced people to reexamine their most basic assumptions about fighting and martial arts. Thanks largely to movies like *Enter the Dragon* and *Fist of Fury*, and acrobatic martial artists like Bruce Lee and Jackie Chan,

Americans truly believed that striking (boxing, kickboxing, karate, kung fu) was the most effective form of fighting and self-defense. When my brothers, cousins, and I moved to the US *en masse*, we tested that theory by issuing the Gracie Challenge. At our academy and at seminars all over the country we invited any and all to test themselves against Jiu Jitsu.

Rorion was my father's firstborn son, and my father had always wanted him to lead the next generation of Gracies, but some of us did not see it that way. He was a competent fighter who would take on the occasional kickboxer, hapkido instructor, or self-proclaimed "kung fu master." However, everyone knew that he needed my brothers, cousins, and above all, me, to fight when the monsters showed up at our academy.

The school was empty, except for me and my brothers Rorion and Royce, when a former member of the Russian Judo team, who also boxed, walked in. It was clear that he had very little respect for us and had come to make a point about the ineffectiveness of what, at the time, was an obscure Brazilian martial art. After he changed into his Gi and stepped onto the mat, he began to warm up. I could tell that he was a champion by the way that he carried himself and moved. After about fifteen minutes of calisthenics and stretching, he walked over to where we were sitting and said, "Let's play a little bit."

I stood up and we grabbed each other's Gis like Judo fighters. I was worried about getting thrown so I was very defensive and kept grabbing his leg. Although we were playing nice and neither of us was using all of our power, he could not throw me and grew frustrated. He finally stopped and said, "You're only defending! Try something!" I told him that I was not going to try to use Judo against a Judo champion, but if he wanted me to use my Jiu Jitsu, we needed to change the rules of the game.

After the Russian agreed to allow me to use takedowns that are banned in Judo, I attacked him like a grappler, and took him down. Once we hit the ground, he turned his back, I choked him, he tapped, then jumped to his feet. "You're good at this grappling shit, but you also said that you like anything goes," he said as he took off his Gi. When he balled his fists and began to posture like he wanted to fight, I took my Gi off and said, "Look, man! You better open your hands because if you hit me with a closed hand, I'll hit you back. Let's just use open hands, there's no reason for us to hurt each other too bad." He opened his hands and said, "Okay! Let's go!"

We squared off, he threw a punch, I countered with a *pissao* kick, then attacked. I got him in a clinch, and when I took him down he turned his back. I began to slap him on the neck, then sank a choke and he tapped again. I stood up and said, "Do you want to do it again to make sure I wasn't just lucky?" "No, no, I'm okay," he replied, then sat down in the corner. He looked depressed, so I walked over to him and thanked him for training with me. "You made me feel like shit, but I still believe in myself," he said. "No! No!" I replied. "You're a great champion. You're just not comfortable with this set of rules. If we were playing Judo, it would have been a different story." The Russian walked out of the academy, and I never saw him again.

Once I proved to an opponent that I could defeat them, I never felt the need to injure or humiliate them. More than anything else, I wanted to convert them to Jiu Jitsu students, especially an already skilled martial artist like the Russian. I was able to convert a number of great fighters to Jiu Jitsu. After experiencing the power of Gracie Jiu Jitsu, American wrestling gold medalist Mark Schultz and MMA fighter Yuki Nakai both became incredibly devoted students of our family's art and went on to earn black belts.

For a time, I was fully committed to helping my family promote Jiu Jitsu in America. I moved to the US and we succeeded beyond anything we could have imagined. While Rorion's vision for promoting Jiu Jitsu was great, he did not know how to bring out the best in people. We were never partners with a shared goal and sense of purpose. Instead, he considered me, my brothers, and my cousins his subordinates and servants. Rorion never led with an open heart and was so intent on controlling and monopolizing Gracie Jiu Jitsu that he even sued members of our family for using their own name to promote their schools.

Once my wife and four children arrived in America, I grew uncomfortable living under my brother's wing. This arrangement was too infantilizing for my wife and me, who had been independent since we were teenagers. Given that I was the family champ and doing most of the heavy lifting on the mat, I decided to start my own academy.

Breaking off on my own was not an easy decision because my father and older brother considered it an act of betrayal. I was not a US citizen and relied on Rorion for my green card and bank account, and this further complicated matters. I made this decision with my heart because I would rather be happy on my own than follow an uninspiring leader. If I do not love what I am doing, I can't be creative, dynamic, and the best that I can be. The older I get, the more I realize that love and passion fuel and motivate me.

Still, Rorion needed me. When he told me that he was putting together America's first *vale tudo* competition in 1992, my heart soared. I thought that my dream to represent my family and Jiu Jitsu in America had finally come true! I thought that this was my opportunity to show my ability and prove that I was a champion. I was stunned and sorely disappointed when he informed me that our younger brother Royce would be fighting instead of me.

When Rorion asked me if I would prepare Royce for the UFC, I did it for the sake of Jiu Jitsu because I was the only member of the family with the experience to coach him for something like this.

Unlike some of our brothers and cousins, Royce was not a Jiu Jitsu champion and had never fought a *vale tudo* bout before the first UFC. Given his youth and inexperience, he would need all the help that I could give him.

Rorion sensed my disappointment and tried to soften it by saying, "If Royce loses, you'll be there to back him up." I did not like his reasoning. If he wanted to make sure that the first UFC was a great success, why not put me in it to represent the family? While my dad and brother claimed that they wanted Royce to represent the family because he appeared so young and unthreatening, that was not the only reason. They could control Royce, but as I had already proven by starting my own school, they could not control me.

I trained Royce for the first Ultimate Fighting Championship. With me in his corner, he won the first UFC tournament and opened America's eyes to the power of Jiu Jitsu. After Royce won the second UFC, many Americans thought that he was the most dangerous man alive.

Royce's success put Rorion on top of the world. He had achieved everything that he had worked so hard for. However, when he tried to take control of the entire Gracie family and chart the course of Jiu Jitsu in America, he made a fatal error. In the beginning, we all stood behind him 100 percent, but over time, Gracie Jiu Jitsu became Rorion Gracie Jiu Jitsu, and then finally Brazilian Jiu Jitsu. Our family is too big and combative to be lorded over by one man. After Rorion did not reciprocate our efforts with gratitude, love, and respect, our family fractured, we were no longer united, and it was every man for himself.

After Royce won UFC 2, he thanked me on television and told the world that I was ten times better at Jiu Jitsu than he was. Nowhere did this comment raise more eyebrows than in Japan, where MMA was already established. Almost a decade before the UFC, Japanese wrestler Satoru "Tiger Mask" Sayama had established the Shooto fighting organization. Although it was not *vale tudo*, Shooto was the first fighting organization to allow both striking and grappling.

I was growing less and less interested in fighting in the UFC and in the US. Instead of a true test of martial arts skill, it was a spectacle of violence whose ads promised "NO RULES." Because Americans had been raised on pro wrestling and Jackie Chan movies, they did not understand fighting and booed every time a fight went to the ground.

Although I enjoyed teaching Jiu Jitsu, surfing California's point breaks, raising my kids, and making new friends in America, after all the training, sacrifice, and hard work, I was burning to fight. Win, lose, or draw, I knew that the time to make my mark in martial arts was now. Even though I never defined myself as a "fighter," I believed that as a martial artist and Jiu Jitsu teacher, I had to fight to validate what I was teaching my students.

The Japanese promoters wanted me to fight in Shooto and it sounded interesting, but they offered me only journeyman's wages. In 1994, the Japanese promoters finally got serious and offered to pay me $50,000 to show and another $50,000 if I won the 1994 Vale

Tudo Japan. The opportunity to fight in Japan was something that I had been waiting for my entire life. Not only would it establish my financial independence; it would restore my pride. It was hard to sit on the bench and watch the world treat Royce like he was the world's greatest fighter when he wasn't even the greatest fighter in our family.

When Rorion learned that the Japanese had approached me to fight in Tokyo, he told me that he didn't want me to fight in Japan. If I did, he said I would be going against the family, and nobody would support me. I decided to go anyway because I knew in my heart that this fight would change my life forever.

Initially I had asked my brother Royce to corner for me like I had done for him in the UFC, but he refused because of my brother's decree. I was disappointed that he did not support me. I had rescued Royce from a full-blown panic attack moments before his first fight in UFC 1. Had I not been there for him every step of the way, I doubt things would have turned out so well. Even though my father and brother strenuously objected to me fighting in Japan as the undisputed family champion, I did not need their permission. I had been successfully taking on all challengers for two decades.

chapter 11

FIGHT CAMP

ONCE I SIGNED A CONTRACT, SET A DATE, AND COMMITTED TO A FIGHT, MY SOLE focus was on my preparation for that bout. I immediately felt the weight of expectations and could not allow this to affect me. I knew that in a few months, only I would be standing in front of a crowd, practically naked, totally exposed, and totally alone.

To win the Japan *vale tudo* tournament, I would have to win three fights in a single night. There was only one formula for success, and that was to leave nothing to chance. For me, the mental process of withdrawing from my friends and family was much harder than the grueling physical protocols of training. Every fighter trains their own way and has prefight rituals that give them confidence. Before a big bout, many fighters withdraw from society and go somewhere without distractions to focus only on their training and their fight.

Muhammad Ali bought land in Pennsylvania and built a gym with a boxing ring, a dining hall, a mosque, and a handful of simple log cabins. Even when he was the world heavyweight champion, Ali slept in a one-room cabin with no electricity or no running water, and used only a fireplace and oil lamps for heat and light. Every morning at 4:30 a.m., a bell sounded and he laced up his combat boots, took a six-mile run in the hills, chopped wood, ate breakfast, and took a nap. After lunch, Ali sparred for an hour and a half and after dinner, played cards and was in bed by 10 p.m.

I did most of my prefight training in Los Angeles and broke it into three six-week blocks. During the first training block, I lifted heavy weights in short sets four times a week. My goal was to break down the muscle tissue, because a muscle grows after its fibers sustain damage, and the body repairs them.

Cardio, my second training block, was always the most agonizing. When I did my cardio, my goal was always to get my heart rate up, then to use breathing techniques to bring it back down as quickly as possible. At least four times a week I ran up the stairs in Santa Monica Canyon, but if I felt up to it, I faced the opponent that I feared most: the sand dune near Point Mugu.

I would run up and down that sand dune fifteen times, and it never got easier. After I sprinted up the dune, my heart rate would get as high as 190. By the time I walked down to the bottom, it was down to 120. Instead of lifting weights four times a week, I now lifted lighter weights and did more reps, twice a week.

During my third and final training block, I lifted light weights twice a week, did shorter cardio sessions three times a week, but now my main focus was Jiu Jitsu. Each morning, I had an intense two-hour Jiu Jitsu training session that consisted of drills, clinching, and submissions. In the evening, I would line up my best students and train with one fresh opponent after another. I didn't wear a Gi so I could get used to the slipperiness of a sweaty body. These were long, controlled sessions, nothing too explosive. My goal was to build stamina, stay sharp, and avoid unnecessary injuries.

Irrespective of the block, I always did my Biogynastica workout routines of stretching and bodyweight exercises. I tried to break up my routines to keep it interesting. Sometimes, instead of swinging on

the rings, I would climb the metal poles that held them up like they were coconut trees. Other days, I walked on the dip bar like a balance beam, then stood on one leg and tried to pull my other foot next to my head.

I never used an alarm clock to wake me up in the morning during training. Instead, I slept for as long as it took for my body to feel fully rested. After I got out of bed, I took my pulse. If my heart was beating at 54 bpm, it was a day to train. However, if my heart rate was 60 bpm, it was a day to rest and recover because I was on the verge of overtraining.

Pushing yourself to your limit is different than overtraining. Sore muscles recover in days, but the side effects of overtraining, fatigue, and frequent illnesses can take weeks or even months to recover from. Many fighters do not realize how much hard training takes out of your body, especially your immune system. It is important for high-level athletes in any sport to keep this in mind, because once your immune system is compromised, it is difficult to maintain your health.

Nutrition was an important part of my fight camps. My meals were 40 percent protein, 30 percent fat, and 30 percent carbohydrates.

Unlike Muhammad Ali, who supposedly celebrated his victory over George Foreman with twelve eggs, two steaks, and ice cream, my diet never had boom-and-bust cycles. I grew up in a family of fighters that followed an extremely strict diet. We pushed our bodies to the limit all day, every day, so the food we ate had to give us maximum energy, digest easily, and never leave us feeling bloated, heavy, or full. Even as small children we were taught that food was a source of nutrition, not pleasure.

More than one hundred years ago, my uncle Carlos Gracie invented a diet that generations of Gracie fighters have followed. He believed that the key to good health and a long life was keeping your blood's pH level as neutral as possible. My uncle's goal was to keep the body in a state of equilibrium by carefully considering what foods, digestively and nutritionally speaking, combined well together. He divided food into categories:

1. Animal protein, vegetables, fats, and oily foods
2. Starches
3. Sweet fruits, fresh cheese, and cream cheese
4. Acidic fruits
5. Milk
6. Raw bananas

There is very little snacking with the Gracie diet, and meals are spaced four or five hours apart so that the body has time to absorb the nutrients each time you eat. As important as what you eat is when you eat and what foods you do, and do not, eat together. For example, if we ate acidic fruit, we did not combine it with any other food. We would never eat two starches, like rice and beans, together. My family never ate dessert after a meal. What fruit and natural sugars we did eat, we ate as a separate meal. The foods we ate were always very healthy, no white flour, sugar, or processed foods.

Because I always had to be prepared to fight, I almost always adhered to the basic protocols of the Gracie diet. When I was getting ready for a fight, I followed a modified version of this diet. I no longer consider the Gracie diet something that is written in stone. Different members of my family have interpreted it differently, and it has served them well. When my son Kron trains for a fight, he eats very little during the day, and then after training, eats two large dinners, two hours apart.

While getting ready for the Japan Open, I began working with a nutritionist. There were times I felt weak, like my body was not getting sufficient nutrition, so I began to eat smaller meals at shorter intervals. Instead of eating three times a day, I ate six or seven. Although I ate beef, I relied more on organic chicken and fresh fish for protein. My breads and cereals were all fiber-rich and multigrain. It is difficult to get all your necessary nutrition from only your food, so the nutritionist added vitamin supplements to my diet as well. I noticed that these changes gave me the capacity to push my body even further during training. Not only did I notice an increase in power, but I recovered faster as well.

I started a typical training day by drinking a great deal of water to hydrate my body because it was not unusual for me to sweat out 2–4 pounds (32–64 ounces) in a single workout. I also wanted my stomach and bowels as empty as possible before training. After my first workout, I would often have a late-morning snack of whole-grain bread with thick slices of white cheese and turkey breast. If I had a midday Jiu Jitsu training session, afterward I ate a late lunch of greens, cashew nuts, steamed vegetables, brown rice, and roasted chicken breast, then drank more water and let my body rest.

Following my last training session of the day, I would stretch, cool down, and take an inventory of my body. I made mental notes of any soreness, strains, or injuries so I could work around them the next day. Finally, for dinner I would eat a five-egg omelet (with only two yolks) and a sweet potato, but if my body craved it, an organic top sirloin steak. Then more water and a good night's sleep.

During my preparation for the Japan Open, weeks blurred into months and before I knew it, I was standing in front of my students, addressing them for the last time before I left for Japan. I could see the pride in their eyes when I told them that they were my inspiration for this fight. I had great affection for my first generation of American students. Not only had their support enabled me to emancipate myself from Rorion, but their confidence in me bolstered my confidence.

As hard as I had trained physically in California, I did my most important spiritual training in Japan. Weeks before my fight, I arrived in Tokyo with my ex-wife, Kim, my son Rockson, and my brother Royler. After we cleared customs, my Japanese manager drove us straight to a house in the mountains near Nagano. Now, I would withdraw even deeper into myself.

My first fight in Japan was so important to me that I got there weeks early to give myself enough time to get completely comfortable and acclimated to my new environment. This did not mean just getting over jet lag; I wanted to connect with Japan on a deeper level by immersing myself in their culture and nature. For me, the most important part of my spiritual preparation was retreating into nature. I believe that the sun, water, air, sand, rocks, trees, and mountains are all living things. Not only do I draw strength and energy from them; they connect me to the larger universe.

During our days in the mountains, my brother, son, and I exercised, ran the mountain trails, and did some low-intensity Jiu Jitsu. Some days, I would wake up not feeling 100 percent and tell my brother Royler, "No training today, I'm going to rest." He was often surprised, but I did not let his expectations sway me. Training for the sake of self-discipline is pointless and superficial to me. I was always very conscious of avoiding unnecessary injuries and do not under-

stand why fighters spar or even train hard close to a fight. The risks
are so much greater than the rewards. Most important, the time for
the hard work is over; it is too late to make any significant gains.

After lunch, I walked by myself deep into the woods and sat down.
Sometimes I would carve a walking stick, but most of the time, I just
stripped the bark off tree branches, then honed them smooth. My only
thoughts were about the blade and the wood. This simple daily ritual
helped me to clear and empty my mind of all distractions. Afterward,
I would go back to our house in the woods and eat a home-cooked
meal of fresh food. With each passing day, I felt more powerful and
grounded in Japan.

Many great fighters had prefight rituals that they felt gave them
an edge over their opponents. Kimura did more push-ups than anyone, and trained longer and harder than anyone. Ali got up at four
thirty to run. Tyson sparred for ten rounds without headgear. I too
had a prefight ritual that boosted my confidence. There was a snow-
fed river near our house, and twice a week, I stripped down to my
Speedos, put on a mask and snorkel, then submerged my entire body
under the freezing water. Submersion in freezing water triggers your

most primal survival instincts. The ice baths that are popular today are a shock to your system, but nothing like this.

The instant my head went all the way under the water, it felt like I was burning alive, while someone was simultaneously sticking ice picks into my brain. At least if you burn, you die fast. When you freeze, you die slowly. Your body's first instinct is to breathe, so getting the panic breathing under control and lowering my heartbeat was always my first and most difficult objective. After about a minute, the pain would pass. When I stepped out of the river I felt warm inside like the power of the universe was inside me.

My final ritual took place the evening before I left for Tokyo to fight. I would go into the woods and light the pile of wood I had collected during my stay on fire. As it burned, I gave thanks for the opportunity to represent my family and Jiu Jitsu, then stared into the flames until they burned out. After that, I was ready.

When I arrived in Tokyo for the prefight press conference and the fighters' meeting, I felt deeply connected to Japan and strangely disconnected from the other fighters. Most of them had just stepped off the plane and seemed unfamiliar with their surroundings. On the day of the fight, I got to the stadium very early and took a nap in the locker room. After I woke up, I gave thanks to God for my life, then acknowledged that today was a good day to fight and, if necessary, die. Next, I exercised, broke a sweat, and got my heart rate up. My prefight warm-up was as much about connecting with my senses as it was about breaking a sweat and loosening my muscles. Once I felt connected, I focused only on my mission and visualized what I was there to accomplish. While victory was my ultimate objective, if I was too attached to any outcome, it could affect my performance in the fight.

Finally, I meditated, then used my breathing techniques to get my heart rate down to 60 beats per minute and waited to be called to the ring. Physically and mentally I felt strong, but also empty, alone, and resigned to my fate. As I made my way to the ring, I felt like my radar was now switched on. I had no plan, no strategy, and no expectations. The engagement began the second I caught my opponent's eye from across the ring. I used my intuition to try to capture his emotions and get my first set of clues. To do this, I let my gut feelings, not my brain and rationality, guide me.

When the bell rang, there were no second thoughts, other than acting without hesitation or mercy. It did not matter if it was an exchange of punches or grappling techniques, my goal was to make my opponent uncomfortable, because this would make him desperate and he would eventually offer me something. It was also important that I remain comfortable and never try to hang on to lost ground. I did this by reestablishing my base, then reevaluating my options.

My opponents that night seemed unprepared and overwhelmed by *vale tudo* rules and the long rounds. Over the course of the next few hours, I defeated a wrestler and two strikers in barely six minutes of total fighting time. After I won my final match and the referee raised my hand, I did not climb the ropes and celebrate like a jackass. Instead, I shook hands with my opponent and bowed to the crowd. I was not about to spoil the moment by acting without martial rectitude. The Japanese fans and I bonded on a very deep level that night. They understood me in ways that I did not yet understand myself. This was one of the greatest moments of my life. Not only had I brought a Japanese martial art back to Japan, but I had used it to defeat all comers. I felt like a lost child who had finally found his way back home.

chapter 12

STAYING ON TOP

ANY CHAMPION IN ANY SPORT CARRIES A GREAT DEAL OF WEIGHT ON THEIR shoulders, because they are the one to beat. Some rely on natural ability, others hard work. What made me different from the other fighters in my family, and I believe one of the reasons that I remained undefeated for so long, was that I always focused on my weaknesses. Even when I was a champion, my mind was never on my last victory, but my next war.

Very little changed in my day-to-day life after I won in Japan. After a short surf trip, I returned to LA and resumed teaching and training at my academy. Now people treated me like a powerful person because of my recent victory in Japan. I did not allow this flattery to affect me. I did not cure cancer or usher in an era of world peace. I was neither a king, nor a saint, and never allowed myself to lose sight of the fact that I was a mere mortal who happened to be good at Jiu Jitsu. I could not allow myself to think that I was somehow more important than others, or I would become what people expected me to be, not who I really was. Being humble and living simply helped me maintain balance in my life, but sometimes this was easier said than done.

If I went to a Jiu Jitsu tournament to watch my son compete, everybody knew who I was, and every few seconds someone asked me to sign an autograph or take a picture with them. Everyone told me how great I was and while this was flattering, it was also dangerous. Any champion who believes their own publicity and hype will not be a champion for long.

In addition to surrounding myself with people who kept me honest, I also developed strategies that helped me keep everything in perspective. If I went to a Jiu Jitsu tournament, as soon as it ended, I went to a crowded public place alone and walked around. Maybe one out of a hundred people would recognize me, but to most people I looked like just another Hispanic in LA.

So many great fighters have a hard time sustaining their greatness. Some get complacent at the top of the pyramid and slack off. Others abandon the strategy and tactics that made them champions. Still some buckle under the expectations of others.

Mike Tyson grew up on the streets and was totally unprepared for what happened when he became the world's youngest heavyweight boxing champion. After he married an actress, he got lost in the world of money and fame. When his coach and father figure, Cus D'Amato, died, Tyson really lost his way. His biggest mistake was replacing his longtime coaches and trainers with a new team who encouraged him to depart from his tried-and-true strategies. Not only did his boxing career fall apart, but so did his life.

Because all fighters have a limited shelf life, my goal was to train and fight smart and extend mine for as long as I could. While I was never reliant on a coach or trainer, I drew a great deal of strength from my family and friends. I was always very conscious and selective about those I wanted around me during a fight camp and at the actual fight. Three of my most important sources of support were my brother Royler, my son Rockson, and my best friend Sergio Zveitler. In the end, they were in my corner for all my fights in Japan.

In my son's case, this was his apprenticeship. Rockson wanted to be a fighter, so I wanted to show, not tell him, what it took to become a champion. We had an extremely close relationship, and the fight camps in Japan drew us even closer together. I looked forward to the day that he would be standing in the ring and I would be in his corner.

Sadly, after I left my brother Royce's corner to focus on my own career, his reign as UFC champ ended. Not only did he fail to defend his title in UFC 3, but after a draw with Ken Shamrock in 1995, he did not fight again for five years. With Royce now out of the picture, my father and older brother Rorion wanted me to fight in the UFC to redeem our family's reputation. By 1995, however, I had absolutely no interest in this American spectacle and only wanted to fight in Japan.

Someday I would be able to sit back and reflect on my fighting career, but that time was not now. It was the time to train and devise new challenges for myself that kept me humble and sharp. Orlando had taught me that the day would come when I would fail, and how I recovered from it would be my ultimate test.

After I won the first Japan Open, I knew that the biggest challenges that I would face as a champion would be mental. I refused to see myself as an undefeated champion. Instead, I constantly handicapped myself and created challenges that kept the taste of defeat in my mouth. Some days I would announce to my students that I was going to limit myself to one specific attack on one specific limb. Other days I would not use my hands, or only give myself a limited amount of time to finish my opponents. When the Jiu Jitsu world champions came to LA for competitions, I opened my academy's doors and trained with many of them. I also had great students who kept me sharp and motivated.

As tough as some of the cops, bouncers, soldiers, wrestlers, and kickboxers who gravitated to my academy were, to find hell and then comfort in it, I often went to the Pacific Ocean. Surfing big waves was one of my favorite ways to test and push my physical and emotional boundaries because it is an exercise in complex problem-solving.

People who have never surfed think the sport is about fun, sun, and bikinis. Nothing could be further from the reality of surfing. Like Jiu Jitsu, it is an incredibly difficult, and at times brutal, sport. When you are learning, there is a hundred times more pain than pleasure. Even after you become proficient, the seconds of joy you experience riding waves are outweighed by hours of paddling and getting smashed by waves.

I grew up in the sea, and there is nothing that terrifies me more than an angry ocean. It has infinite power and is too powerful to fight head-on. When I fight, it is only against another man. If I am smart and precise, at some point, I will find an opportunity to impose my will. No man can create the same level of panic and discomfort as the ocean.

If the surf got big in California, I used to drive north to Rincon Point, home to some of the longest, most perfect wintertime waves in California. When the conditions are right, it is possible to ride one wave for hundreds of yards. One winter, a huge northwest swell hit the coast, and I decided that it was a good day to test myself. I stood nervously at the top of the point with my board under my arm. Paddling out on these days required as much strategy and timing as it did physical strength. During a long, interval, wintertime swell, the Pacific Ocean is like a boxer. It delivers its fury in flurries of waves called sets. While there might be as many as a dozen waves in a set, there are also long intervals between them, called lulls.

I jumped off the rocks, and the second my board hit the water, a riverlike current swept me south toward the river mouth, where the waves broke with maximum ferocity. Even worse, my timing was bad, and there was a big set on the horizon. The first wave broke way beyond me. I tried to hang on to my board, but the wall of white water easily ripped it out of my hands. Although I was attached to my board by a urethane cord called a leash, I could not retrieve it, because I was too busy diving under mountain after mountain of white water.

By the time I recovered my board and resumed paddling, I was way at the bottom of the cove. Now I had to paddle against the current to get back to the river mouth where I could catch a wave. The whole time I was paddling, I watched older guys in hooded wet suits riding big, old-fashioned, single-fin surfboards. They were not flashy, but they were calm, precise, and beautiful to watch. While I was scared and having to work to manage my fears, men who were much older and weaker than me were playing and having fun.

Finally, I reached the river mouth, and even though I was exhausted from the long paddle, I was determined to ride at least one wave. In waves this size, you must commit 100 percent to catch one. When a set approached, my focus became sharp. I paddled for the first wave with total commitment. Once I felt the wave lift me, I jumped to my feet. The drop was long, and when I saw the wall forming way in front of me, I turned too soon. In a millisecond, my heavenly vision of a hundred-yard ride turned into a nightmare as the offshore wind got under my board and the lip of the wave and I became one.

A cubic meter of water weighs roughly a ton. This wave was at least fifteen feet tall, so tons of water landed on me and pushed me deep into a violent cloud of churning white water. My leash stretched tight, then suddenly went slack, and my heart sank because I knew that I had lost my surfboard.

I finally surfaced, got a quick breath, and then had to dive under more white water. Finally, there was a lull and I began to hyperventilate in order to get as much oxygen into my bloodstream as possible. My problems were multiplying fast. The current was sweeping me toward the seawall, and I had only a seventy-five-yard window to reach shore. If I didn't, I would either have to try to climb the seawall without getting smashed against it, or swim another half mile south and reach shore at La Conchita Beach.

My thought process was similar to the one that many fighter pilots use to make decisions in combat. Called the OODA (Observe, Orient, Decide, Act) Loop, pilots first observe the situation they are facing. Next, they orient themselves by accepting reality and consider their options. Then they decide on a course of action and, finally, act with total commitment.

I was close to my physical limit, so I decided to take decisive action and swam into the impact zone, the area where the waves break, with full force. If I had just remained in deep water diving under waves, not only would I have exhausted myself, I also would not have made it to shore. It sounds counterintuitive, but there are times in surfing when you have to use the ocean's power to your advantage, even if it means taking a few waves on the head.

The first large wave that broke in front of me sent me cartwheeling underwater toward shore. Thirty seconds and another beating later, my feet touched the rocks, and I was able to get in before I hit the seawall. Although I only caught one wave, my feet got cut, and I took a beating, I felt a great sense of accomplishment. After disaster struck, I stayed calm, suppressed my feelings of panic, came up with a plan to get to shore, and successfully executed it. My ability to remain calm in the eye of the storm would soon be tested again.

chapter 13

WALKING MY TALK

IN 1995, I SUCCESSFULLY DEFENDED MY TITLE IN THE SECOND JAPAN OPEN. AFTER defeating three opponents in one night for a second time, I told the Japanese promoters that from now on, I would only fight single bouts. Although they agreed and paid me more than any other MMA fighter at the time, they also insisted I only fight Japanese fighters.

In addition to training, I was now spending more and more time with doctors and physical therapists. My list of injuries was growing. My back, hips, neck, and shoulders were wearing out and these injuries reminded me that I was not going to be able to fight forever.

After I defeated Japan's most popular wrestler, Nobuhiko Takada, in 1997 and again in 1998, they pitted me against Japan's biggest MMA star and my toughest opponent yet, Masakatsu Funaki. He had previously defeated Bas Rutten and both Shamrock brothers and was a decade younger and forty pounds heavier than me. Funaki was a seasoned warrior and a formidable opponent.

My prefight routine was always the same. I had my main training camp in Los Angeles and then returned to the same cabin in Japan weeks before the fight. There I would acclimate, withdraw, and spiritually prepare for the fight.

When I returned to the Tokyo Dome in May 2000 to fight Funaki, I knew that this was going to be a war. Funaki would later say that he did not see this as an MMA bout, but a *kakutougi* fight instead. Much more serious than MMA, in *kakutougi* there is no referee or doctor's stoppage, and defeat can mean death. My opponent did not even allow his cornermen to bring a towel to throw into the ring to stop the fight.

After the fight started, we clinched and wound up in the corner, exchanging punches and knees. Funaki was mainly focused on preventing me from taking him down. Nine minutes into the fight, he grabbed my neck, then attempted a guillotine choke. This was my opportunity to drag him down to the ground, so I took it. We hit the ground with Funaki on top of me, and as I was establishing my guard, he hit me with a right that broke the orbital bones in my eye socket. Suddenly, I had no vision. Funaki did not realize the extent of my injury and popped right back up to his feet and began to kick my legs.

Now my psychological base was every bit as important as my physical base. Above all, I could not let my opponent know how badly I was hurt. My primary goal was to preserve the distance between us so that he could not land a head kick or knockout punch. Every time Funaki kicked me in the legs and feet, sixty thousand Japanese fans roared. I absorbed the punishment and tried not to get swept away by the contagious emotion of the crowd. I could not allow my ego to override my brain.

When I remembered Orlando Cani's words, "All athletes fail; what separates the greatest from the great is their ability to recover from failure," my perspective suddenly changed. I no longer saw this as a disaster, but rather a once-in-a-lifetime test of my martial arts skills. Now I felt strangely calm, like this was the challenge that I had been training for my entire life. I considered my options because my next strategic decision would make me or break me. My brother was screaming, "Stand up! Stand up!" If I stood up, Funaki might not know that I was badly injured, but I would be fighting blind. If I stayed on the ground and made no effort to stand up, he would know that I was injured, but would still not know the extent of my injuries. To do this, I had to let Funaki kick me more than thirty times. Although this situation was not ideal, it bought me the time to recover. I spent more than a minute on my back, and as I was devising a strategy to fight blind, some of my vision returned.

Funaki's unanswered flurry of kicks had made him complacent, and when I saw how close he was, I kicked his knee and this gave me the distance to stand back up. Now on my feet with some vision, I wanted to finish this fight as quickly as possible. Because Funaki knew I was hurt, I didn't think that he'd expect me to be aggressive, so I attacked. I used kicks, then knees to set up a takedown, established the mount position, and began to punch Funaki in the face with hard rights and lefts. After I trapped his arm, he was basically defenseless, and I continued hitting him with brutal rights that split open his brow. Funaki's courage never wavered.

When I saw the dazed look on his face, I knew that it was time to finish the fight, so I transitioned to his back and began to choke him. Even in this hopeless situation, Funaki refused to tap. Like me, he would rather die than surrender. The referee didn't stop me; I stopped myself when I felt Funaki's body go limp. When my opponent eventually regained consciousness, he later said that he was

filled with joy, because he was still alive. Funaki was a valiant warrior who forced me to draw on all my martial arts skills to defeat him. Above all, I was very impressed by his heart.

Acceptance, faith, hope, and patience allowed me to keep the feelings of panic and fear from overwhelming me. I never lost my mental base and made the kind of desperate decisions that lead to defeat. Because Funaki did not realize how hurt I was, he didn't capi-

talize on his window of opportunity, and it closed. There are times in life when there are no good options, and you must choose the least worst one. Thankfully, Orlando Cani had taught me that one day I would fail and would need to trade the attributes of the lion for those of the ultimate survivor, the rat. I thought that this would only be temporary. Little did I know that this would be my new reality and I would never be the lion again.

chapter 14

FREE FALL

FIGHTING IS, BY NATURE, AN UNUSUALLY LONELY AND SELFISH OCCUPATION. FOR decades my focus and the focus of those around me was on me, my health, my training, my diet, or my next fight. In retrospect, I can see that I put off many important things because I did not value or recognize the importance of time.

November 25, 1981, was one of the happiest days of my life. My ex-wife, Kim, gave birth to our first child, Rockson. My heart soared when I realized that my son would be part of the fourth generation of Gracie fighters. Before he could walk, I moved his tiny legs and arms and began to prepare him for a life of action the same way that my father prepared me.

As Rockson began to grow, he reminded me of my dad, because he was small, restless, and always on the go. Even as a child, he was incredibly coordinated and fearless. My son rose to every challenge that I put in front of him. He hung from ropes, did tricks on the trampoline, rode a skateboard, and of course, learned Jiu Jitsu.

Just like me, Rockson wanted to be a great Gracie fighter and follow in my footsteps. He spent his formative years as a Gracie in

Rio at a time when street fights, school invasions, and challenge matches were regular events. More than my other three children, Rockson was raised like me, by the Gracie wolf pack. Not only was he a regular presence at some of the most famous academies in Rio, at seven years old, he watched me fight Hugo Duarte at Pepe Beach.

Rockson and I first moved to America before my wife and other children. Although he was extremely athletic, by American standards he was small, and this made him insecure. Once he realized that the Black kids were the toughest kids at his school, he ran onto their basketball court, grabbed the ball, got into his first of many fights, and I got the first of many calls from the principal. What I didn't know at the time was that these regular displays of reckless courage endeared him to some of his classmates who would go on to become gang members.

Given the growing popularity of Jiu Jitsu in America because he was my son, Rockson carried a great deal of weight on his shoulders. He embraced this challenge. By the time he was nineteen, Rockson had won three Pan Am Games titles and was one of the leaders of the next generation of Gracie fighters. Still, this was not enough for him. Skateboarding, surfing, or picking fights at parties—it didn't matter the activity—he pushed the limits way beyond anything reasonable and rational.

Like me, Rockson did not see the point of school because he only wanted to fight and teach Jiu Jitsu. He was a skilled and dedicated student of our family's martial art, and always performed at the academy, so I turned a blind eye to his misbehavior. There were warning signs that my son was on the wrong track, but given my own involvement with gangs and drugs in Rio, I figured that this was a phase that he would pass through. Although my father always offered his advice, he allowed all of us to make our own decisions even when they were bad ones, and I did the same thing with Rockson.

In addition to Jiu Jitsu, my son was also a successful model. In the fall of 2000, Rockson moved to New York City with his model girlfriend to work. I approved of this decision and thought that a change of scenery would do him good. New York City was the epicenter of the modeling world, and my cousin Renzo had an excellent academy there where he could train.

Once Rockson and his girlfriend arrived in Manhattan, he called to tell us that everything was going well. I did not hear from him again for over a month and began to worry, so I asked Renzo to track him down. After my cousin learned that Rockson had split up with his girlfriend, then vanished without a trace, he feared the worst.

Renzo reached out to a student who was a New York City police officer. He checked the hospitals, then went to the morgue and found a postmortem photograph of an unidentified person who had died of a suspicious drug overdose in a cheap New York City hotel. The policeman recognized him by a tattoo that read "Rickson Gracie, world's greatest dad." I was heartbroken when my older brother Rolls died in a hang-gliding accident in 1982, but nothing could prepare me for the death of my firstborn son. In early February 2001, I flew to New York City alone, confirmed for myself that Rockson was gone, and returned to LA with his ashes.

Shortly after Rockson's memorial, the Japanese promoters offered to pay me five million dollars to fight Kazushi "The Gracie Killer" Sakuraba. This was more than any other MMA fighter had ever earned at that time. This Japanese MMA fighter had already defeated my brothers Royce and Royler and my cousins Renzo and Ryan. Because of Sakuraba's victories over them, once again I was the Gracies' last line of defense. Now I had to be brutally honest with myself. Representing my family was my raison d'être, my purpose in life, but now I did not know if I ever wanted to fight again. My fight against Funaki had been an all-out war. Both of us fought to win that night and left everything in the ring. To defeat him, I had to use all my martial arts resources to recover from a disaster that would have brought defeat had I mishandled it.

That fight was the ultimate expression of my martial artistry. If I was now just going to fight for the money, I would no longer be a martial artist. I lived according to a personal code that was not dissimilar from the Bushido code (courage, rectitude, mercy, politeness, honesty, honor, loyalty, and character), and the Japanese fans understood and respected me for this. There was a point when I felt like I was the Gracie most qualified to represent Jiu Jitsu, but the truth was that after Rockson's death, I no longer did.

Deep in my heart, I knew that it was time for me to quit and to clear the ring for the next generation of Gracie fighters. Given my emotional state and the emotional state of my family, I decided to pass on the most important fight of my career. Although there would be many offers to fight in the coming years, I would never fight again. I had not just lost my son, I had also lost one of my closest friends and greatest sources of inspiration. Going back to Japan and fighting without him in my corner was unimaginable. Even more crushing was the thought that I would never get to stand in his corner and watch him represent our family and carry on our traditions.

Although Kim, our children Kauan, Kaulin, and Kron, and I stuck together and supported one another as best we could, all our hearts were shattered. After we lost Rockson, everything fell apart. When my children began to heal and get on with their lives, his death hit me the hardest. I was steamrolled by feelings of irretrievable loss and felt like I was stuck in a bad dream that I could not wake up from. The pain was greater than anything I had ever experienced. I no longer had a sense of purpose and didn't care what the future held, because my life had become a sad, joyless existence. Surfing, Jiu Jitsu, my friends—none of it held any interest for me. I felt no excitement, hope, or joy about anything.

Nothing could dull my pain and I didn't even try to hide from or fight these feelings. I no longer cared about my image, my undefeated record, my fame, or even my life. I was bleeding inside and not embarrassed if people saw me bleed. For some, talking helps, but for me, I needed to grieve alone. There were times when I felt like my grief was passing, then another wave of sadness would wash over me. As I grew more depressed, my injuries and personal problems continued to accumulate and grow.

I had not only lost a piece of my heart and soul, I had lost my appetite for life. I stopped trying to get over Rockson's loss and doubted that I ever would. I now felt like I was lying at the bottom of a lake with a big stone sitting on my chest. The longer I stayed down at the bottom, the less I wanted to resurface. There were times when I wanted to die.

At my lowest moments, I would retreat to a stand of trees at the high point of my property in Pacific Palisades and pour out my grief. If you look at a tree superficially you don't see the details, much less the animals and ecosystem that the tree supports. When I moved into my house in Pacific Palisades, I befriended a group of blue jays that lived in my trees. I like blue jays because they are smart, loyal, and brave birds. They mate for life, and if a hawk or cat invades their habitat, they band together and attack it. I began to leave the birds peanuts and, over time, they got used to my presence.

At first they were just friendly, but with the help of peanuts, we connected. There was one blue jay who got confident enough to eat out of my hand. Eventually I was able to put a peanut in my mouth, stand on my lawn, lift my arm, and he would land on my arm, walk down to my shoulder, and take the peanut from my mouth. He became a good friend and we looked forward to seeing each other. I could always recognize my friend because he had a different pattern on his wing.

One day, my blue jay friend showed up with another blue jay. The second that I saw them together, I felt the same way I did the first time my son brought a girlfriend home to meet me. Shortly after that, they built a nest right above our front door, and soon they were teaching their offspring how to fly. I was honored that they chose to raise their family with our family. At one point there were five or six blue jays living there.

There was one especially large pine tree on my hillside. One day I decided to climb high into that tree. As I got close to the top, I had a clear view of the Pacific Ocean, and decided that was where I would build a memorial to my son. After I bought the wood, nails, and other supplies, I felt motivated and hopeful for the first time in many years. Every morning, when I climbed the tree to work on the memorial, my blue jay friend would fly over, say hello, and tell me what had happened in the tree during my absence. Now that I was in his domain, we grew even closer. As I put hammer to nail, then sandpaper and varnish to wood, the fog of grief slowly began to lift.

When I finally finished the memorial platform for Rockson, I mounted a framed photo of him, looked out to the sea, and said, "Rockson, you're with Rolls, and all the others that I have loved. I still have things to do and need to get on with my life." Shortly thereafter, without warning, all the blue jays were gone and I took this as a sign. Sad or happy, depressed or not depressed, the cycle of life would continue with or without me. It was time for me to do something meaningful with what remained of my life.

My first wife, Kim, and I fell in love when we were nineteen and bonded in a very special way. Having a strong woman by my side to support me allowed me to focus on my Jiu Jitsu and put my energy into my quest to become the greatest Gracie. After we married and started a family, my focus shifted to my children and providing a strong foundation for their lives. I was an imperfect husband and before we moved to America, Kim and I separated and the future of our marriage was in doubt.

Although we were able to repair the marriage and form a strong and successful team in the US, after Rockson's death, like many couples who lose a child, we drifted apart. I no longer wanted to live in California, fight, or try to maintain the fiction of omnipotence and invincibility. I knew that if I was ever going to find inspiration again, I needed to get back to my roots in Brazil. I asked Kim for a divorce, gave her all of my physical property, and went home.

I will never get over the loss of my son, but after three years of intense grief, depression, and mourning, I reevaluated my life. Recently, a close friend's son died. When I reached out to console him, he told me that he had been thinking a lot about me because I was one of the only people who could understand the pain that he was feeling. We cried together and poured out our sorrows for our sons who left us too soon. Afterward, I told him to embrace the unfathomable sadness. Only time, hope, love, forgiveness, and acceptance could help him make the passage to the next stage of his life. Eventually, he would come out the other side, but he would never be the same person again.

The Japanese continued to try to entice me back into the ring with big paydays, but I knew in my heart that this part of my life was over because I could no longer represent Jiu Jitsu in the manner that I saw fit. While I will never get over the pain of losing my first son, hope, patience, and my physical practices allowed me to find comfort in darkness and move on with my life. After a struggle that was worse than anything I faced in the ring, I came out the other side a scarred and changed man, but committed to a new life of service.

chapter 15

TEACHING JIU JITSU TODAY

BECAUSE OF MY OWN FIGHTING CAREER, I HAD NEVER BEEN ABLE TO DEVOTE 100 percent of my energy to teaching Jiu Jitsu. Now that I knew I would never fight again, I wanted to dedicate my life to spreading my family's martial art. In 2008, I moved back to Rio to begin a new life, and teaching Jiu Jitsu was at the center of it.

The martial art of Gracie Jiu Jitsu was originally developed so people could defend themselves in the real world. A century later, a large percentage of the Jiu Jitsu population has gravitated to an athletic, rule-bound sport also called Jiu Jitsu. While this new version still requires skill and stamina, it is oddly impractical for self-defense. Even though this variant is divorced from the martial art, I respect the athletes who practice it because we share many of the same values. They are tough, competitive, train hard, and accept the inevitable injuries that come with the sport.

In several of the academies I visited, I watched world champions trying to teach students of all athletic abilities variations of moves that take years of practice to understand, much less execute. It was beautiful to watch, but reminded me of primates who had learned our martial art. What they were teaching was incomprehensible and irrelevant to 99 percent of the people in the Jiu Jitsu world.

At my seminars, I encountered devoted students and dedicated teachers who did not know Jiu Jitsu's litany of base, engagement, connection, leverage, and timing. Some could mask these deficiencies with strength and athleticism and still capture arms, crank a neck, and sink a choke, but they had never been exposed to Jiu Jitsu's mental, physical, and spiritual trinity. Many of today's sport Jiu Jitsu champions have never fought *vale tudo* or MMA. Black belts can't teach self-defense if they've never learned or even been exposed to it.

Recently, a present-day sport Jiu Jitsu champ reached out to me for a private lesson. He is a tough competitor who regularly wins at the highest levels of competition—Gi, or no Gi—it does not matter. The Jiu Jitsu champ knows everything there is to know about grips, sweeps, and hooks. I didn't need to teach him any techniques, only the larger concepts. Before our first class, "engagement" and "connection" were not part of his vocabulary. While he is a great athlete, he is not yet, in any sense, a martial artist.

The Jiu Jitsu champ had a great offensive guard, but when his opponent started to pass it and he was forced to uncross his feet, he went immediately to defense. I showed him how to use his calves to maintain the same amount of pressure on his opponent after his guard was opened. This small detail was eye-opening to him. He said, "It changed everything."

I only gave the Jiu Jitsu champ one class before he left to compete. After the tournament he called me to tell me that not only had he won, but he had submitted opponents using what I had taught him.

Since then, he has returned for more lessons. I've been teaching him how to breathe, about connection, weight distribution, and pressure. Given all the blood, sweat, and tears that he has invested in Jiu Jitsu, he deserves to have a much deeper understanding of it. The Jiu Jitsu champion's new knowledge of the trinity and litany has supercharged his performance. It was the missing link. He is now on the path to becoming a martial artist.

A strong, athletic person can replace precision and technique with physicality, but a small, weak person does not have this option. In Hélio Gracie's conception of Jiu Jitsu, you never force anything. Instead, you first establish an impenetrable defense, then wait for your opponent to make a mistake and then capitalize on it. Although I was never weak, my Jiu Jitsu was never built around strength. No matter how strong I got, there was always going to be someone stronger. As I got better and better, I tried to minimize my use of power and instead focused on the invisible aspects.

It is much easier for me to teach someone how to be a high-level Jiu Jitsu competitor than it is to teach them how to be a martial artist. There are so many more variables in the martial art of Jiu Jitsu. You need to know how to defend against punches, elbows, knees, head-butts, not to mention eye gouges and bites. You must be able to use every tool in your arsenal without mercy or hesitation. The headbutt, for example, is a lethal weapon. Ten pounds of weight delivered with the crown of the head to a person's face can be devastating. If someone sticks their finger in your eye or bites you, what are you going to do? A martial artist's decision to engage or not engage should be governed by their survival instincts, not their ego. Physical confidence enables you to walk away from unnecessary conflicts. This, in short, is Invisible Jiu Jitsu.

When dealing with aggressiveness and negativity, I try to deflect it with positivity. Years ago, my brother Royler and I were driving in

Rio on our way to go surfing. It was hot and the traffic, even by Rio standards, was bad. I cut off a taxi and the driver started screaming and cursing at me. I leaned out the window and said, "Sorry, have a nice day." Royler is a volatile guy and he was stunned! "Rickson! Why didn't you kick his ass?" he asked. I responded, "Royler, we are on our way to a beautiful beach to go surfing, and the taxicab driver is going to battle traffic all day for a little bit of money. He is miserable enough already. Why should I add to his misery?" Sometimes a situation requires compassion instead of aggression.

Aggression is often born of insecurity, and insecurity is the product of ego, fear, anger, and above all, an insecure state of mind. When dealing with people ruled by these irrational forces, I try not to respond in kind. I often apologize even when I am not wrong to diffuse a potential conflict. I don't care if someone thinks that I am a coward. I know in my heart that I am not and have nothing to prove to them, or anyone else. My goal is to live another day, not to get shot or knifed by a jumpy teenager for egocentric reasons. Defeating an adversary is less important to me than remaining at peace with myself, even if it means negotiation and compromise instead of conflict. Sometimes this is easier said than done because it requires the discipline not to let your own ego or emotions get the better of you. To do this successfully, you draw more on your mental strength than your physical strength. While you have to act decisively, you also have to act proportionally.

I am more afraid of a teenager who grew up in the ghettos of Rio or LA than I am of any professional fighter. They don't give a fuck that I'm "undefeated Rickson Gracie," because most of them have the great equalizer—a gun. Guns and knives take you to the limits of your martial arts possibilities. Even the best MMA fighters and martial artists, me included, don't have foolproof defenses against them. It only takes five pounds of pressure to pull a trigger and end a life.

Any coward, even a child, can do this, and there is nothing honorable about it. A bullet will cancel out my lifetime of martial arts training and kill me just like anyone else.

In situations of armed conflict, your brain is one of your most powerful weapons, because a martial artist who is mentally, physically, and spiritually present can act and react, engage, or disengage, depending on what the situation requires. There are so many variables in a street fight or a random attack that you have absolutely no control over. Does your opponent have a concealed weapon? Are they mentally unstable? Are you outnumbered? Do they have a communicable disease? You cannot anticipate these things, only manage them as they arise.

I want my students to be prepared for anything. When I taught policemen or soldiers, I'd pick up a club, approach them, say, "Good morning, sir!" and then take a swing at them. I did this to make them comfortable with the chaos, unpredictability, and uncertainty that play such a big part in any real-life conflict. As important as a martial artist's ability to fight is their ability to remain calm in any storm.

Over the years, I have used a more extreme tool, cathartic discomfort, to force some of my more advanced students to face their demons. Although the process can be unpleasant, it takes them way beyond what they thought were their limits. Coyote, my friend and longtime student, was a very tough and creative Brazilian fighter. However, he relied too much on speed and used to get very claustrophobic. One day, we were training hard, and about twenty-five minutes into our session, I got on top of him. When I put my chest on his face, I could sense that he was beginning to panic. I figured that there was no better time for him to face his demon, so I increased the pressure.

Coyote struggled for a minute, then really began to panic and said, "Okay, let me go!"

"No! We just got started," I replied.

"GET THE FUCK OFF ME OR I'LL NEVER SPEAK TO YOU AGAIN!"

"Then don't ever speak to me again."

Next, Coyote got serious and tried to fight me. Desperate to cut this painful process short, he struggled with all his might. When he finally exhausted himself, I said, "Only think about breathing." He realized that he had no choice, and finally began to breathe. As my friend's panic began to subside, I coached him through the movements necessary to escape.

Coyote's five minutes of darkness were transformative. Afterward, he said, "That was the most important lesson of my Jiu Jitsu career. The nightmare you put me through was unbelievable. I thought that I was going to die! When I realized that I had no way out and started to breathe, the nightmare passed. My position did not change, but I had to get calm enough to survive before I could escape."

By finding comfort in hell and surviving this agony, Coyote rid himself of a larger agony that had hindered his Jiu Jitsu progress for years. Without this brutal physical lesson, he never would have progressed. Afterward, my student could relate a feeling with the knowledge necessary to solve a problem that he had been avoiding for years.

While some in the Jiu Jitsu community consider my obsession with fundamentals old-fashioned and antiquated, my son Kron competed and won at the highest levels of sport Jiu Jitsu using basic, but perfectly executed, Jiu Jitsu techniques. After Rockson died, Kron devoted his life to the martial art. Because he was my son, he too had a bull's-eye on his back. He not only handled the pressure well—Kron seemed to thrive on it. Before he received his black belt, he won two Jiu Jitsu world championships, four Pan American Games, and fifty-one matches in a row by submission. After Kron won the most prestigious competition in grappling, the Abu Dhabi Combat Championship, he decided that he wanted to fight MMA.

I respected Kron enough to let him follow his own path in MMA. When he decided to train with the Diaz brothers, I became more of an observer than a coach. While I don't think that there are any tougher fighters in MMA, I do not share the Diaz brothers' fighting sensibility because it is built around toughness and a willingness to endure punishment in order to hand out punishment. I always wanted to win quickly, decisively, and avoid getting injured whenever possible.

chapter 16

MODERN MMA

THE FIGHTING ENVIRONMENT I WAS MOST COMFORTABLE IN WAS ONE WITHOUT weight divisions, time limits, rules, or cages. In these situations, you must draw upon the full extent of your martial arts abilities. When you fight without weight divisions, your opponent might spend the whole fight on top of you. I always accepted the fact that I had to survive for long periods of time waiting for my opponent to make a single mistake.

Modern MMA is not like this. All of the fighters today are tougher and better prepared to fight in any range. Strikers train to get back to their feet. Wrestlers want to ground, pound, and beat their opponents into submission. The short rounds and emphasis on action have put Jiu Jitsu fighters at a disadvantage, because they can no longer afford strategic patience. This has happened because the UFC built their rules around fans, not fighters.

After the UFC deemed ground fighting "boring," referees became quick to stand fighters up when a fight went to the ground. As a result, if a grappling technique did not work quickly, fighters gave it up, even if they were in a good position. The cage also became the third man in the ring. If you do not know how to fight inside it, you are at a great disadvantage. This forced MMA fighters to build strategies around a piece of equipment. Worst of all, the UFC added judges who, like judges in all sports, make subjective and sometimes questionable decisions. None of my fights ever went to judges. If they had, I would have felt like I had lost for that reason alone.

If I were an MMA fan, I would want a conclusive ending, not one in which both fighters think they won because they ran out the clock and their fight was decided by judges. In a three-round MMA fight, say Fighter A wins rounds one and two, but in round three he gets thrown on the ground, mounted, punched in the face, and is getting choked unconscious when the final bell rings. Who wins? Fighter A, because he landed a few punches in the first two rounds? If so, these metrics for success are disconnected from the martial arts reality of who would have lived or died in a real fight. There was a tennis match at Wimbledon in 2010 that lasted over eleven hours! If tennis has tiebreaker rounds, why not MMA? Fighting is about survival—kill or be killed. Today's MMA fighters are all complete, but the rules of engagement diminish their ability to fight smart, technical fights.

Modern MMA, especially the UFC, is about entertainment. More than anything else, fighters are rewarded for standing in the center of the ring and slugging it out. Performance-enhancing drugs, short rounds, and the cage have made physicality as important as technique. A fighter can lose and still be rewarded a fifty-thousand-dollar bonus for "The Fight of the Night," because their bout was bloody, brutal, and action-packed. There is no meaningful criteria for "The Fight of the Night" other than the opinion of a promoter who has only stepped into the cage to wrap championship belts around fighters' waists. The UFC has become a place where martial artists go to get reincarnated as "entertainers."

How can anyone be considered a champion without a legitimate pyramid of contenders, and decisive victories? The UFC has created a fighting culture that has more to do with spectacle than sport. It does not surprise me that a boxing mismatch between Conor Mc-Gregor and Floyd Mayweather Jr., or a YouTuber and pro basketball player, or a possible MMA fight between two middle-aged billionaires are what fans want to see today. While it's financially smart for promoters and fighters to capitalize on the public's ignorance, these mismatches degrade both boxing and MMA. I accept this sad reality but I will not be surprised if men will soon be fighting gorillas or packs of hyenas like the Roman gladiators once did.

Instead of spectacles of violence, I would like to see honor and martial artistry return to fighting in the form of a weeklong, single-elimination *vale tudo* competition that pits truly elite fighters, Olympic and world champions from the combat sports (wrestling, Jiu Jitsu, Judo, boxing, kickboxing, and MMA), against one another in bouts with as many fifteen-minute rounds as necessary to determine a winner. To level the playing field, I would get rid of the gloves and judges and replace the cage with a raised platform. In addition to strict testing for performance-enhancing drugs, referees would not be empowered to stand up fighters on the ground. The fighters would fight only once a day, and all of the competitors would be carefully monitored by doctors with unilateral power to disqualify them due to concussion or injury. Rather than ring girls, celebrities, and drunken fans, the audience would be small, invitation-only, and mostly composed of distinguished martial artists. Take away the judges, points, gloves, cage, and short rounds, and resilience, breathing, continuity, comfort, discomfort—the things that will save you in a real fight—become important again.

As entertaining and novel as an event like that would be, *vale tudo* and MMA are far less important to me now than teaching Jiu Jitsu to regular people to rehumanize them by awakening their senses from their cyber slumber. Technology has disconnected people from their intuition and their primal selves. If I can bring them back into their bodies, I can teach them to trust their senses, not just their brains.

chapter 17

REHUMANIZATION THROUGH JIU JITSU

WE ARE NOW BOMBARDED WITH SO MUCH STIMULI THAT THE MODERN MIND IS A kilometer wide, but only a millimeter deep. Smartphones, video games, and social media are all about instant gratification. Attention deficit hyperactivity disorder (ADHD) is a sign of our distracted times. Worse, the simple things that once gave people happiness—friends, family, the respect of your peers—no longer do. Technology cannot help you appreciate wonderful, human things like raising a child, or having meaningful relationships. To do this, you have to be present, and this requires sensitivity and perception.

Many kids today don't express themselves physically. Instead, they choose to be avatars in the virtual universe. Social media makes many reluctant to accept the reality of who they really are. If they only show themselves in the most flattering light, only talk about their successes, but never their inevitable failures, the gap between the reality of their life and the illusion of their life grows. It is possible to become a world champion virtual athlete, quench their sexual thirst, order their meals, and find companionship, all without leaving their rooms! They can even design an AI girlfriend to their exact physical and emotional specifications. Ultimately, this adds to their insecurity and leaves them fragile when it comes to facing and dealing with the realities of life. While we all have expectations, ultimately we must face and accept what life presents us with.

Even worse is the culture of virtual violence that it has created. It does not surprise me that most mass shooters are isolated, alienated young men. An unusually large number of them are single and have no close friends. The internet is full of websites that show real murders, bombs landing on civilians, and mob beatdowns as entertainment. People have grown accustomed to watching and outsourcing violence to the police, soldiers, and private security companies who do it in their name. Wars are much easier to support when you don't have to fight them yourself. Some want to blame American gun culture, and others want to blame mental illness for our increasingly callous and violent society. These are broad and vague explanations that ignore the larger questions about our disembodied, dehumanized culture.

If you only live on the screen or out of an Amazon package, you are not engaging most of your senses. Jiu Jitsu can help to cure this imbalance by pulling people out of their world of make-believe and forcing them to face who they are and who they are not. Take the issue of transgender athletes. I respect anyone's decision to live their life as a transgender person. I accept whatever anyone considers their gender identity to be, but draw the line at men competing against women in Jiu Jitsu and MMA, especially when there are risks to physical injury due to marked differences in strength.

While transgender women (women born biological males) have been very successful in female sports, transgender men (men born biological females) have not succeeded in male sports. Not one transgender man has competed successfully against men in Jiu Jitsu, MMA, or any other sport that I know of. There is a simple solution to this dilemma: create a separate category for transgender athletes irrespective of their gender identities.

I see the same magical thinking when it comes to the recent attempt to normalize obesity and act as if a person's diet and lifestyle have nothing to do with it. Today, the US military cannot reach its recruiting goals because so many young Americans are overweight and ineligible as a result. Food is fuel that keeps us alive, and that fuel must be burned. If you eat 4,000 calories a day, work long hours sitting at a desk, then go home and stare at a screen, this is a recipe for obesity and bad health. People all over the world are suffering from diabetes and heart disease in record numbers. Obesity is now a bigger world health problem than hunger.

In the West, especially the United States, when people get sick or injured, they expect, even demand, a drug or medical procedure to address the symptoms of their problem. If you have type 2 diabetes, high cholesterol, and high blood pressure, it is much easier to take a pill than to stop eating red meat, ice cream, and fast food. Changing your diet and lifestyle does not just require self-discipline; it also forces people to take an active role in their health. While a pill might affect the symptom, it does not address the root cause: an unhealthy diet and lack of physical activity. If you don't treat yourself from within, you will dig yourself into a hole that you can never get out of.

There is no better example of this than America's opiate crisis. Today many people are choosing not to feel anything. Instead, they live in an opium dream. Legal or illegal, heroin, fentanyl, and oxycodone all have similar effects on humans. They kill both physical and mental pain. I understand the desire to numb yourself all too well. If you lose a child, like I did, there is no escaping the searing and irrational pain. I too dulled my pain with drugs and alcohol. However, not only did I wake up the next day feeling awful, but I was still heartbroken.

For many years the American medical profession prescribed addictive opiates very freely and recklessly. In many cases, when patients can no longer get or afford prescriptions, they turn to illegal opiates like heroin or fentanyl. The facts speak loudly for themselves. Last year, more Americans died from drug overdoses, over 100,000, than died in the Vietnam War and War on Terror combined, and there is no end in sight.

I feel fortunate that I grew up in a very different world. For those of us who were lucky enough to come of age during the post–World War II era, we led charmed lives during a golden age. We enjoyed unprecedented security and prosperity. Many people, especially Americans, believed that they were above the fray. Now that sense of security and eternal prosperity has been ruptured by the COVID lockdown, political instability, and the possibility of world war. Instead of focusing anger on the leaders and institutions that have failed and betrayed them, Americans are turning on each other.

As a Brazilian who grew up under a military dictatorship in a society riddled with corruption, I have a very low opinion of career politicians and even lower expectations of them. I have never allowed politics to enter my academies. I always wanted them to be sanctuaries, places where students could escape for a few hours a week, and be judged only by what they did on the mat. Thanks to Jiu Jitsu, I sit in a unique and privileged position, because the mat is one of the last totally level playing fields. Prince, gangster, business titan, champion wrestler—they are all the same. This safe space enabled people with absolutely nothing in common to get to know one another without judgment or preconceptions.

North, South, East, Midwest, and the West—I love America. I have traveled to more parts of this country than most Americans in the thirty years that it has been my home. I have taught Jiu Jitsu to people of every race, class, gender, and walk of life and never has a single student said to me, "I can't train with him because he is Black,"

or "I can't train with him because he is gay." In fact, the opposite usually occurs. More often than not, people with absolutely nothing in
common realize that they have more in common than they ever imagined and become friends.

Learning Jiu Jitsu is a hard and honest process that requires honesty and hard work. If you do the work, you can gain courage and
peace of mind. The changes do not come overnight, and the cure does

not come in a pill form. It begins by facing the fact that life is not always fun, people are not always nice, and you do not always get what you want or deserve. Defeat, hardship, obstacles, pressure, and disappointment are things that, sooner or later, everyone experiences. For some things, like the death of a child or a spouse, the only cure is time, patience, and hope, and these are important elements of Invisible Jiu Jitsu.

chapter 18

JIU JITSU FOR EVERYONE AND ANYONE

AS MY INSPIRATION AND PASSION FOR TEACHING JIU JITSU RETURNED, MY BODY fell apart like an old car. My neck, back, and hip were simply worn-out. Often I went directly from teaching a seminar to the physical therapist's office for treatment. I was in constant pain and tried to will myself through it, but I eventually had to accept the fact that Father Time had come to collect a long overdue debt.

After a hip-replacement operation, I recovered quickly and saw how much the mindset and habits I had acquired from my lifetime of martial arts aided my physical rehabilitation. My diminished state also made me realize how unwelcoming modern Jiu Jitsu is for weak and insecure people. I understood why 90 percent of Jiu Jitsu students quit as white belts.

Instead of throwing beginners to the sharks in open classes, my father used to make them take private lessons before they trained with anyone else. By the time his students set foot in an open class, they had a solid grasp of Jiu Jitsu's trinity and litany. It made me sad that the weak, the very people my father and uncle invented Gracie Jiu Jitsu for, were being ignored, and I wanted to change that.

Although I lost the physical ability to fight due to my injuries, I have grown as a teacher. In the old days, my pedagogical method was "follow the leader." I used my physicality to show my students how to execute moves. It was all very practical, kill or be killed. I now see Jiu Jitsu differently. I am not just teaching a martial art; I am adding something to a person's life. When I work with beginners, my goal is to guide them to new frontiers of consciousness that will allow them to find some measure of physical and mental comfort in any situation.

As my father taught me, a student's needs are more important than a teacher's expectations. No matter the student's talent, athleticism, or lack thereof, my father was a patient and positive teacher. His goal was always the same, even when the progress was slow. The teacher has to be there—mentally, physically, and spiritually—to help and support them every step of the way. To Hélio Gracie, Jiu Jitsu was always about solving the problems, managing stress, and feeling comfortable in uncomfortable situations. His hope was that his students would take the lessons they learned in his academy and apply them to every aspect of their lives. It was more important to him that his students won in life than on the mat.

I can teach base, weight distribution, engagement, connection, and breathing with very little stress. As my students get familiar with these concepts, I teach them how to respond reflexively. Instead of combatants, we are training partners, there to help each other sharpen our skills. When I swing the pool noodle at someone's head to make them duck or swing it at their feet to make them jump, their mind gets sharper, more deliberate and decisive. When I am teaching someone how to deflect and redirect blows, I am waking them from their physical slumber. In just a few lessons, students learn how to better sense danger, understand the difference between patience and passivity, and know that losing is not the same as being defeated.

When I teach a student for the first time, I take stock of them as an individual because I teach the entire person. I use physicality to reveal things that most people can hide in their daily lives: their state of emotional balance, their irrational fears, their natural aggression or passivity. The physical questions that I pose allow me to look under the rug and see who a person really is, not who they would like me to think they are. Someone can look strong on the outside because they have large muscles, but often those muscles are psychological armor, and beneath them lurks a small, scared person. On the other hand, someone can appear skinny and weak, but can have the heart of a warrior. I really don't know who I am dealing with until I apply some physical heat.

After I take stock of a student, I design and build a curriculum to help them in a profound way. If they are passive, I push them. If they are aggressive, I calm them. If they panic, I teach them how to face and manage their personal demons. If a person can tap into the trinity and litany of Jiu Jitsu, they can reconnect with their primal self.

Over time, people who train in Jiu Jitsu learn to play like lion cubs. To an outsider, they appear to be fighting, but they are really just sharpening their claws and instincts. While most humans never have to fight another person, much less kill, they still need to be able to handle stress, control pressure, and seize opportunities.

Learning to breathe, physically engage, detach, and disengage also forces people to be present and interact with other humans. If students do this work honestly and diligently, they don't just get better at Jiu Jitsu; they can rebuild themselves as stronger people—not just in a fight, but also in their physical, mental, and spiritual lives. Now I look at my students not as athletes, but as people trying to confront and overcome problems. As I am educating their movement, I am also changing their mindset. My goal is for them to develop a proactive mindset that leads them to confront their problems directly.

If you push your opponent and they resist, you must immediately make adjustments, and try to take advantage of their energy. This sensitivity to change and capacity to feel instead of just act will allow you to flow with ever-changing situations and capitalize instead of just reacting. If I am fighting a tug-of-war with someone, I will pull the rope, but when my opponent pulls back, I'll drop the rope and they'll fall on their back. I don't just want to be effective, I also want to be efficient.

I engage students' curiosity by showing them the invisible power of base, connection, and leverage. This alone gives them a feeling of strength that many have never felt. If you lift weights in the gym or go to a yoga class, the number of variables is much smaller and less dynamic than in Jiu Jitsu. In powerlifting, you need weights, a bar to hold them, and physical fortitude to push past pain and exhaustion. In yoga, you stretch, strain, move, and breathe, in a very choreographed way, but nobody is on top of you, trying to choke you. Both lack the counters and checkmates of Jiu Jitsu that force you to try to hold your emotions in check, control your fears, and use your physicality.

It is more important for me to teach someone how to survive than it is to teach them how to win because I want them to feel like they can face anything and maintain their mental integrity even under great pressure. We all need support networks and points of reference to grow. Jiu Jitsu gives people a form of practical support and a therapeutic practice that forces them to be present and engage.

Invisible Jiu Jitsu is less about learning a huge range of techniques than it is about recognizing what emotional state you are in, using breathing techniques to remain calm, and devising a strategy to avoid, minimize, or settle a conflict. It can be as simple as: your adversary moves in direction A, then you move in direction B. If you are forced to engage, you connect, defend, deflect, and escape with the goal of survival. If your goal is only to survive and live another day, Jiu Jitsu becomes much simpler. If you are not a pro fighter, you don't need to spend years learning how to defend and counter every possible attack. If a 100-pound woman survives an attack by a 250-pound man and walks away with a few bruises or a bloody nose, she has won.

Years ago, I gave private lessons to a man who had a conflict with a professional athlete who was 6'2", 220 pounds, strong as an ox, and probably on steroids. My student was twenty years older than his adversary and forty pounds lighter. He was once a good athlete, but he now worked long hours at a desk job and accepted the fact that he probably couldn't win this fight. Nonetheless, he refused to live like a coward and hide from his antagonist. I respected him for this and devised a strategy for him to fight to survive.

More important than this strategy was the fact that he walked into my school and began training. By doing this, he confronted his worst fear and gained confidence. Every class, I would morph into his tormentor and do my best to bully and intimidate him. After a few months, something shifted inside of him, and I believe his adversary sensed this. Just because you are big, buff, and can hit or catch a ball does not mean that you know how to fight. After training with me for six months, my student reached out to his foe. They met in person, resolved their differences without fighting, and became friends. Much more important than teaching chokes and armlocks is teaching people how to incorporate martial arts concepts into their daily lives.

chapter 19

INVISIBLE JIU JITSU

I ONCE HAD A STUDENT WHO WAS A RECOVERING ALCOHOLIC. HE USED TO SAY, "JIU Jitsu: cheaper than a psychiatrist, and more fun than AA." He was only half joking, because Jiu Jitsu had given him principles to apply to his life and an external support system to stiffen his spine when he felt weak. I have proudly watched many of my students take the physical knowledge that I have taught them, apply it to other parts of their lives, and go on to do great things.

When I first met Jiu Jitsu master Pedro Sauer, he was a skinny guy who drove like Ayrton Senna and wore sunglasses, day or night. I knew that he had boxed and trained in Tae Kwon Do and Judo, so I invited the fifteen-year-old Pedro to train with me and my nine-year-old brother Royler. It was such an eye-opening experience for Pedro that from that day forward, he devoted himself to Jiu Jitsu. Eventually he earned his black belt and college degrees in economics and business. He was a successful stockbroker in Brazil when he decided to move to America and help spread Gracie Jiu Jitsu.

In addition to being a great teacher, Pedro was an absolutely fearless warrior and a frontline soldier who fought to prove the effectiveness of Jiu Jitsu. He weighed only 150 pounds, but after the first UFC, a 250-pound bodybuilder challenged him to a bare-knuckle *vale tudo* bout. Even though he was giving away 100 pounds, Pedro accepted the challenge and beat the man in a tough fight. His use of the guard impressed even Hélio Gracie himself. Today, Pedro heads his own Jiu Jitsu association and has schools all over the country.

Sergio Zveiter was finishing up law school when he began to train with me in Rio. We met just a few months before my first fight with King Zulu, and he traveled to Brasília to support me. Afterward, he told me that he thought I was going to get destroyed and was amazed that I was even willing to fight King Zulu. "Winning," he said. "I thought that was impossible." My victory showed him that there were no limits to the possible.

Initially he wanted to learn more about conflict and self-discipline, and how he could use this knowledge in his professional life. Sergio's father was Brazil's Minister of Justice and at a very young age he was a top lawyer at one of Rio's biggest law firms. Like me, Sergio had a great deal of weight on his shoulders and represented powerful clients in big cases.

No matter how busy Sergio was and how important he became, from my first pro fight to my first trip to Japan to my last fight with Funaki, Sergio was in my corner. He has been one of my greatest sources of support over the years. When we met, we were both on track to do big things and as we accomplished them, we were always there for each other with love and support. Ours has been a great friendship because we were never competitive. Instead we always tried to elevate and improve each other.

My cousin Jean Jacques Machado is one of the most inspiring people in Jiu Jitsu today. Born with only a thumb and part of a pinkie on his left hand, Jean Jacques had no time to contemplate his disability because he was raised by the Gracie wolf pack. Called "5-1" because he only had his first and fifth digits on his hand, he was mercilessly teased for his birth defect, but he never saw himself as anything other than our equal. What impressed me most about my cousin is the way that he transformed his disability into an ability and developed an intensely personal and creative style of Jiu Jitsu. He learned how to adapt and improvise better than anyone I have ever seen in my life. Because his left hand had almost no fingers, it was easier for him to slide it under people's chins to secure chokes or pry away arms. He pioneered the modern style of Jiu Jitsu that is so common today in no-Gi Jiu Jitsu and MMA. Instead of competing against me like his older brother tried to do in 1986, Jean Jacques decided to learn from me instead. As a young teenager, he would take the train into Rio from his home in Teresopolis and spend entire days watching me teach private lessons, observing and absorbing every detail.

Jean Jacques Machado was one of the most successful competitors in the history of grappling. In addition to winning the Brazilian Jiu-Jitsu National Championships for eleven consecutive years, he won the most prestigious competition in grappling: the Abu Dhabi Combat Championship. Irrespective of his success as a fighter,

Machado also made an equally gigantic mark as a teacher, coach, and leader.

Many celebrity martial artists who run schools are more figure-heads than teachers, but not Jean Jacques. He teaches most of the classes at his school himself and takes a great personal interest in his students both on and off the mat. Negativity is forbidden in his academy; his students are not allowed to use the word "can't." He teaches his students how to find a way, however big the problem. It is great to become a champion; it is an even greater thing to help people reach their full potential. Jean Jacques once said that the biggest difference between an ordinary man and a warrior is that the warrior sees everything as a challenge and the ordinary man sees it as either a blessing or a curse. Like me, Jean Jacques believes that Jiu Jitsu is not only a martial art, but a way of seeing life with better, sharper vision.

Peter Maguire, the coauthor of this book and *Breathe*, was a skinny surfer finishing his PhD when he first showed up at the Pico Academy in 1992. After I learned how powerful his family was, I was impressed by how radically, confidently, and unequivocally he followed his heart. He chose a life of service instead of the one of wealth and comfort that he was born into. Some go through life without guiding principles and willingly trade their freedom for wealth, status, or security. Peter refused to live this way.

As I got to know him better, I saw similarities between our personal situations. Despite all the family pressures and dramas, we both remained happy and in control of our respective destinies because we were much stronger than our adversaries. Instead of hatred in our hearts, we had pity for our respective adversaries and antagonists. He never altered his course or had second thoughts, and neither did I.

Both of us took chances in 1994 and were rewarded. I went to Japan to fight and Peter went to Cambodia to investigate and document war crimes. In both of our cases, we put everything behind us and never looked back. Although he is regularly called on by governments, statesmen, nongovernmental organizations, and others for his opinion on human rights matters, Peter never lost sight of what was important to him. He always put his family, friends, and public service first.

From Cambodia to Western Australia to France, he was also a great Jiu Jitsu missionary. The 150-pound professor opened many skeptics' eyes to Jiu Jitsu's power and then converted them into students. He still surfs, trains, and teaches his own distinct style of Jiu Jitsu today.

Years ago, Peter walked into the Pico Academy after a trip to a foreign country and he showed me pictures of two demolished trucks. "If I hit the brakes or swerved, I was dead," he said. "I realized that my only chance at survival was a head-on collision. My truck became a disposable survival tool. I floored it, we hit headlight to headlight, I got blasted in the face with broken glass, but survived."

That story made me proud as a teacher, because Peter had applied the martial arts concepts I had taught him so seamlessly during a life-or-death situation. On the surface, this was a car accident that had nothing to do with Jiu Jitsu, but it had everything to do with Jiu Jitsu. Peter controlled his emotions, visualized the outcome he wanted, and executed his strategy with total commitment. This is, in short, Invisible Jiu Jitsu.

chapter 20

THE FIGHT OF MY LIFE

TO BE COMPLETELY HONEST, WHEN I WAS DIAGNOSED WITH PARKINSON'S DISEASE it was not a big surprise. For more than a decade, I have not just been in extreme pain. I also felt like I was aging at an accelerated rate. It wasn't just that my body was breaking down. My motor skills and reflexes were also deteriorating and slowing to the point that I had to give up surfing and hard Jiu Jitsu training. After my diagnosis, I set out to learn as much about Parkinson's as I could because I wanted to engage the disease like I had once engaged opponents in the ring. To do this effectively, I had to learn as much as I could about my new opponent.

Second only to Alzheimer's disease as America's most common neurodegenerative disease, Parkinson's disease is a brain disorder that afflicts more than a million Americans today. Medical researchers think the disease is a result of both genetic and environmental factors. Many people have asked me if it is a result of fighting, but I don't think it is.

Parkinson's is especially hard on athletes like me, because it affects the central nervous system. The condition affects people differently. Some lose their mobility; others only get tremors. The symptoms— muscle stiffness; poor reflexes; loss of balance; depression; difficulty talking, swallowing, and chewing; skin problems; urinary issues; and constipation—get worse over time and there is no cure.

The tremors that come with Parkinson's are a result of damage to, or a loss of, the dopamine-producing cells in the brain. Like serotonin, dopamine is one of the brain's "reward" chemicals. It is released when you have an orgasm, complete a difficult task, smell your favorite food, and do other pleasant things. Dopamine is also a chemical messenger that nerve cells use to send signals to different parts of the body to execute different tasks. Without it, the human body cannot move and function properly. Most of the drugs used to treat Parkinson's disease attempt to raise your brain's dopamine levels. However, these are strong drugs that mostly address the symptoms and can affect your overall health.

After speaking to the doctors and studying the science of the disease, I wanted to talk with someone who has been living with Parkinson's. I remembered that before I told anyone about my diagnosis, my old friend and student Fernando Fayzano asked me, out of the blue, if I had Parkinson's disease. When I asked him why he wanted to know, he said that his friend Winston had Parkinson's disease, and had watched a video of me teaching and suspected that I had it too. I told Fernando that I had tested positive for the disease and asked him if he could introduce me to his friend.

Despite having Parkinson's disease for two decades, Winston still competes in tennis and water polo and leads an active, happy life. When we spoke on the phone for the first time, he told me that my life was not over, but it would be different now. He offered an analogy that I have used ever since to visualize my condition. "Think of it like this," he said. "You are still in the driver's seat of your life. But now you have an unruly passenger who is trying to get in the passenger seat. First, he'll try to change the radio station. If you let down your guard for even one second, he'll grab the wheel and drive you off the road. You can't let your guard down for even a second!"

After I spoke with Winston, I wanted to take the fight to my body's "unruly passenger." When I began to plot my strategy, the first thing that I wanted was a better doctor. To me, the medical establishment's view of Parkinson's disease was overly rational and only two-dimensional. There is much more to a person's physical health than just their body temperature, pulse rate, and blood pressure. I could not trust, much less place my life in the hands of, a doctor who has no interest in me as a person.

It was nothing personal; the American doctors who initially diagnosed me were skilled, knowledgeable, and perfectly nice people. The problem was that I felt no connection with them. Most just marched into the examination room with clipboards in their hands, read my vital signs off a sheet of paper, and barely looked up. I was only a number to them, not a person.

I felt like they were leading me down a one-way, dead-end street that ended in the cul-de-sac called death. To follow risk-averse doctors was to trade my sword and shield for the shovel that I would use to dig my grave. We are all eventually going to die; I accept this. Death is not the issue; the real issue is how we accept death.

Given the stakes of this conflict, I needed to feel a real connection with my doctors because medical professionals are now like my coaches and cornermen. I consult with them constantly and seek their advice on any physical changes I feel, my diet, and exercise protocols. I leave nothing to blind faith or luck.

Winston introduced me to a Brazilian doctor who describes Parkinson's disease as a syndrome, not a disease. A disease is a health condition with a clear and identifiable cause, but a syndrome produces symptoms without a precise reason why. The first American doctor had me taking the pills he prescribed three times a day. My new doctor thought I was taking way too much medicine and put me on a much lower dose. Now I take only one pill in the morning and one in the afternoon. I also use CBD oil and other natural remedies to help stabilize my tremors. The Brazilian doctor told me that I was fortunate that the tremor was my only symptom so far. My hope is to stop taking the medicine eventually. This is obviously very ambitious, but I must have hope.

During the summer of 2023, I went on my niece Kyra Gracie's podcast in Brazil to talk about Invisible Jiu Jitsu and why it is so important to me today. I explained to her that Invisible Jiu Jitsu was about empowering the weak by giving them more courage and confidence. After we discussed now-familiar themes like using Jiu Jitsu to help people find power in their everyday lives and the dehumanizing effects of technology, we began to talk about Orlando Cani. When Kyra asked me if I was still practicing Biogynastica regularly, I told her that it was difficult for me now. Not just because of my back and hip injuries, but because of Parkinson's disease. I did not go on Kyra's show intending to announce this to the world for the first time, but it is not something that I am embarrassed about or trying to hide.

"I'm ready for anything in my life," I explained. "I accept life and what I've done, so I'm happy today." I told her that this neurologic condition had opened my eyes to my age; but not much else had changed in my life. "I don't see it as a surprise," I added, "but as another gift from God to see what I'm going to do about it."

Then I asked Kyra if we could take a break so I could show her some of the basic principles of Invisible Jiu Jitsu. Although my niece is a Jiu Jitsu professor and former world champion, she is also a sensitive and intuitive person. Kyra got it immediately, and afterward, she said that she felt like she was learning Jiu Jitsu all over again.

Parkinson's has also provided me with an opportunity to serve as an example and point of reference for others with it and other terminal and life-changing diseases. I truly believe that God has given me a situation I can transform for the good. My lifetime of training and fighting has made me realize that the most important thing that Jiu Jitsu does is plant the seed of courage in a person. When that seed sprouts it does not mean that they will be ready to fight in the UFC, but much more important, they will be better equipped to face life's challenges.

After that interview, no less than one hundred Brazilian doctors reached out to me. No medical insurance, no copay, no bullshit, just, "Hey, Rickson, I've worked with Parkinson's patients my entire career, and I'd like to help you." If that was not enough, thousands of people, everyone from old students and friends to complete strangers, called and messaged me with their blessings. I can't describe the inspiration and energy that I have drawn from this outpouring of unconditional love and support. Not only did it touch me, but it also made me feel like I'm on track to do something much larger with the rest of my life.

I was surprised that my admission of human frailty touched so many people. The experience left me feeling that it was time to make lemonade out of the lemons that life had given me. Now I am not just a Jiu Jitsu professor. I am a sick person battling an incurable disease and must walk my talk of acceptance and finding comfort in darkness. This does not rob me of the capacity of being happy. We are all going to die one day, but being unhappy, uninspired, and having no love in my heart is a fate worse than death.

Recently I did a long, virtual consultation with Lair, one of the Brazilian doctors who reached out to me after my announcement. Like any good teacher or coach, Lair was frank about my situation and did not flatter me. He asked me a detailed series of questions about the water I drink, the food I eat, the environment where I live, and the unresolved conflicts in my life. I felt an immediate connection with him because his more holistic approach to Parkinson's disease focuses on the things that are under my control that can improve my condition. Instead, he told me that I am in a situation that could go either way and that it was up to me to choose the direction.

A few days after our virtual consultation, new Parkinson's medications arrived in the mail. When I contacted Lair to ask how much I owed him, he said, "This is not about money. I admire you and want to help." Again, this was an act of love. This doctor entered my life to help me with no agenda and he speaks to me in a deep and profound way. This was not just two-dimensional medical guidance from a guy in a white coat. I respect and trust what he says not just because he is a doctor, but also because he has a large, open heart. His nutritional, spiritual, and psychological guidance feels like a gift from God.

chapter 21

COMFORT IN DARKNESS

AFTER LAIR TOLD ME THAT INFLAMMATION KILLS THE BRAIN CELLS THAT RELEASE dopamine, I wanted to do everything in my power to reduce the sources of inflammation in my body. Inflammation is a very broad term for the body's defense mechanisms against viruses, infections, and other injuries and it comes in many forms. If you twist your ankle, it swells. If you burn your skin, it hurts and turns red. These are all forms of inflammation.

Lair told me that one of the biggest sources of inflammation is environmental toxins. They are in our food, water, and many of the items that we use or come into contact with every day: nonstick cooking pans, food packaging, house cleaners, waterproof clothing, carpet, paint, furniture, floss, even certain types of toilet paper. These items contain microscopic, man-made chemicals that take thousands of years to break down and have been linked to diseases like Parkinson's and cancer. Although these toxins are nearly impossible to avoid, I am now trying to protect myself from the worst of them.

As the world has gotten more and more polluted, this has compromised both our food and drinking water. Some of the water in America contains toxic "forever chemicals" (polyfluoroalkyl substances or PFAS). Where I live in California, the water is extremely acidic. This was an easy problem to solve. Now I filter all the water in my house and only drink ionized water.

Animal proteins can also cause inflammation, so my days of eating meat will soon be over. This is a difficult choice, but reducing inflammation is more important to me than the sensual pleasure I get from eating a delicious barbecued steak. Now, if it is not good for me, I don't eat it. If I am serious about this fight, I have to make these hard, but necessary, changes in my lifestyle.

In addition to these defensive measures, I am going on the offense against Parkinson's disease. Instead of just treating the symptoms, like my tremors, I want to address what many believe to be the cause of Parkinson's: the loss of dopamine in the brain. I am now trying to prevent the death of the dopamine-producing nerve cells.

Neurologists have found clumps of proteins in the synapses of the brains of people with Parkinson's. Like debris stopping the flow of water in a river, in this case they stop communication between the cells. Recent studies have shown that fasting might help repair this problem because it puts the body in a state of autophagy, a physiological process that helps the body rid itself of, repair, and recycle damaged brain cells. Each cell contains thirteen parts. Over time, these parts stop working, and the old and damaged cell parts are discarded through the process of *autophagy* ("self-eating"). I am now fasting one day a week. I eat my last meal of the day at four in the afternoon and don't eat again until the same time the next day. If fasting might be able to help repair my damaged brain cells, why not try?

I have also designed new exercise protocols to combat Parkinson's disease. Now I bike outdoors, swim, and play Ping-Pong to improve my hand-eye coordination. I am doing more explosive exercises like plyometrics, and I am still teaching Jiu Jitsu a few days a week. Again, taking an active role in improving my health requires discipline. If I am not willing to make these hard decisions, then I'm just passively allowing my problems to grow and Parkinson's disease to thrive.

I recently went to an American doctor whom I trust and like very much. I was seeing him for the first time in six months for coordination and movement tests. Afterward, he said that my body was still extremely stable and asked how much medicine I was taking. When I told him, he was surprised and said, "That's it? I'm impressed." I informed him of the changes I had made to my diet and lifestyle, and he said, "Officially, I can't offer a professional opinion, because I don't know much about alternative cures." Then the doctor added, "Unofficially, keep doing what you're doing, I'm very proud of you. You are the first person I have ever met who is trying to beat this disease. You have a good mindset and are much happier than most of my patients."

I believe that my mindset is every bit as important as the medical protocols. Cancer, cholera, or Parkinson's disease, I won't let a disease redefine me and the way I lead my life. Say you get cancer; you undergo chemotherapy, and it goes into remission. Instead of being happy that your cancer has retreated, you choose to live in a constant state of fear, because there is a chance the disease might come back. I refuse to live in fear. I can choose to see only the negatives of the situation, or I can see the glimmers of hope. Instead of focusing on what is wrong with me, I focus on doing the most I can with the time and energy that I have left. Illness should not make you terminally unhappy; it just gives your life a new, tighter deadline. Until I reach that deadline, I want to use my time in the most positive and constructive ways possible, not worrying and speculating about things that are out of my control.

Many people facing a serious illness quit without fighting, because they do not have the tools or perspective to engage the challenge they are facing. Jiu Jitsu gave me the strategy and tactics I use to engage and fight Parkinson's disease. Once I knew that I had a life-changing medical condition, acceptance became very important, because there was no getting around the fact that my life was never going to be the same. Timing also became critical because I could not afford to let Parkinson's disease dig its claws into me any deeper than it already had.

My psychological base is especially important now because I need to make careful, informed decisions about my health. I can't let my expectations, doubts, worries, or emotional distress set me back. Although I will consider and try alternative approaches that are outside of the scope of Western medicine, that does not mean that I will ignore medical science and search for miracle cures. Instead, I balance the two and consider anything within reason that might help me.

If I let Parkinson's disease redefine my life and become the focus of it, I will feel defeated and desperate. Instead, I visualize a lifelong fight with the unruly passenger in my car. To keep him out of the front seat, I will use all of the tools that Jiu Jitsu has given me. It is just another fight. Parkinson's can take my life, but it can never take my will. Just like when I fought in the ring, I would prefer to die than to quit.

I am inspired to heal myself, but if I am not going to heal, I am at least going to stabilize my condition as much as humanly possible. Whatever the outcome, the small, day-to-day victories that I win bring me hope because I am taking the fight to the disease. No matter how bad my symptoms get, I will never allow "victim" to become my identity. I'm still teaching and inspiring others by showing them, not telling them, that they can be happy and positive whatever their circumstances. You don't have to be a martial arts master to do any, or all, of this. Anyone can apply Jiu Jitsu's mental, physical, and spiritual trinity, not just to disease, but also to their life.

I am on a good road now due to the changes that I've made in my diet and lifestyle. I lead a humble life and am very fortunate to have another strong woman by my side. When I met my second wife,

Cassia, in Rio, I was no longer young. I had not expected true love, friendship, and passion to return to my life, but they did. My expectations for this relationship were very different because I did not want to repeat the mistakes of my youth. Parkinson's disease has provided a stress test for our relationship and Cassia has passed it with flying colors. As I face my new limitations, she has stood by me every step of the way. Sometimes it is difficult for me because she takes an almost parental interest in my day-to-day activities, but I am extremely lucky to have her in my life.

Today I get great joy out of simple things like cooking, eating, and spending time with my family and friends. The squirrels, blue jays, raccoons, skunks, peacocks, hawks, and crows who have befriended me and live in my yard bring me a sense of peace and connect me to the natural world. I am inspired to be the first person to ever recover from Parkinson's disease. I will probably never reach this goal, but having it and the hope that comes with it have changed everything.

It's a new phase of my life; an opportunity to rise above and lead by example. Although I have had to slow down, I'm still the same warrior. My killer instinct is intact. Even though I am on a new battlefield, my strategies and tactics are the same. The more I think about getting Parkinson's disease, the more I begin to see it as my final challenge from God.

LEARNING TO LOVE MY OPPONENTS

MY DOCTOR, LAIR, ASKED ME IF I HAD ANY UNRESOLVED CONFLICTS IN MY LIFE AND suggested that I resolve them. Although the results have been mixed, it made me feel good to take the first step. As I look back on my life, I realize how grateful I am to my former adversaries like Masakatsu Funaki, Yuki Nakai, Hugo Duarte, Sergio Pena, my brother Rorion, Nobuhiko Takada, King Zulu, and others because they prepared me for my final battle. We had plenty of drama and conflict in our youth, but we didn't just beat each other up in vain. I learned important things from all of them.

After our fight, an emotional Funaki apologized to his fans and said that because he considered this fight *kakutougi*, there were no rematches or second chances, and announced his retirement. I heard that he had taken the loss hard, and I was concerned about him.

When we spoke a year or so later, he thanked me for the fight and said that it made him reevaluate his life. Funaki told me how honored he was to fight me, and I said that the honor was mine. Anyone who was as deadly serious about, and committed to, his mission has my utmost respect. Today he is coaching the next generation of Japanese fighters.

Yuki Nakai, whom I fought in 1995, showed me what the heart of a true warrior looked like. He stands only 5'6" and weighs just over 150 pounds, but by the time he fought me in the finals of the Japan Open, he had already won two very tough bouts against much bigger men. His first match against 6'5" Dutch kickboxer Gerard Gordeau is probably the most brutal bout in the history of MMA. Although the Dutchman was a martial arts champion, he had also worked as a bouncer for many years. This experienced brawler treated MMA like a street fight. When my brother Royce fought him in the first UFC, Gordeau tried to bite the top of his ear off!

During their fight in the Japan Open, Yuki went for a heel hook and Gordeau stuck his thumb so deep into Yuki's eye socket that he permanently blinded him in the right eye. Not only did Yuki continue to fight for the next twenty minutes like it never happened, but he eventually caught Gordeau in a heel hook. Yuki could have easily destroyed the kickboxer's knee, but as soon as Gordeau tapped out, he released the hold instead.

Afterward, Yuki Nakai did not drop out of the tournament, seek medical attention, and try to save his eye. Less than an hour later, he fought an American wrestler 100 pounds heavier than him, survived a vicious ground and pound attack, and submitted him with an armlock. By the time Yuki faced me in the final, both of his eyes were swollen shut and his nose looked broken. Despite these injuries, he was screaming in the hallway, "Rickson! I'm coming for you!" and was truly excited to fight me. Against the advice of my cornermen, I hit him as little as possible, submitted him as gently as I could, and did only what I needed to do to win. Yuki was the real modern samurai that night.

After the Japan Open, Yuki dropped out of MMA because he could no longer see punches coming. He hid his blindness for a long time because he did not want to add to the sport's already bad reputation. With MMA no longer an option, Yuki Nakai opened his heart to Jiu Jitsu and embarked on a very specific mission: he wanted to restore its prominence in the pantheon of Japanese martial arts. In 1997, two weeks before the most important competition in Jiu Jitsu, the *Mundials* (world championship) in Brazil, the doorbell rang at my cousin Carlos Gracie Jr.'s apartment in Rio. When he opened it, Yuki was standing in front of him holding a small bag that contained his two Gis and little else. My cousin had once said to Yuki in Japan, "If you are ever in Rio, look me up," and here he was. Although he spoke neither Portuguese nor English, and did not have a place to stay, he had flown from Japan to Brazil to compete. For the next two weeks, the toughest academies in town opened their doors to Yuki Nakai, and one of his biggest fans and supporters was my cousin Carlson Gracie.

After Yuki returned home, he continued to train, competed, earned his black belt, and opened a Jiu Jitsu academy in Tokyo. By the late 1990s, he was growing increasingly troubled by the ways in which technology was disconnecting people from one another. Above all, he worried that live, in-person communication between individuals was disappearing and being replaced by mobile phones and the internet. Like me, Yuki no longer saw Jiu Jitsu as a martial art that was the sole provenance of warriors, but a form of communication that transcended technology and even language. As Yuki pointed out, no matter the color of your skin, or the language you speak, people become friends in Jiu Jitsu without even talking. "Martial Arts Communication" is his school's motto, and I am very proud that my picture hangs on the wall of his academy. Yuki Nakai is one of Japan's national treasures.

Hugo Duarte, whom I fought on the street in Rio, was the embodiment of courage. It took a lot of guts for a no-name fighter to challenge me in Brazil at the height of my power, then demand a rematch. I have a lot of respect for Hugo for the depth of his commitment to martial arts. He went on to fight some of the toughest men in MMA, including Mark "The Smashing Machine" Kerr. Although he lost, Hugo went three rounds and, as always, fought with all his heart. Hugo, the tough and stubborn fighter I squared off against decades ago, has grown into a coach, leader, and enlightened martial artist.

Sergio Pena was one of my most serious Jiu Jitsu rivals and probably came closer than anyone else to beating me. When we faced each other in a tournament in 1981, I could sense that he truly believed, 100 percent, that he could beat me, and he almost did. He was way ahead on points, but I was able to submit him toward the end of the match. Shortly thereafter, Sergio dropped out of competition and became an airline pilot. I felt bad for him and was not sure if I had crushed his dreams, or if this was just part of his evolutionary process. In either case, I was happy to learn that he is now living in the US and teaching Jiu Jitsu. Sergio is not only a great teacher, but he knows what it takes to win.

Despite our disagreements, I also have a great deal of love and gratitude toward my older brother Rorion. Without him, Jiu Jitsu would never have taken the world by storm, and I would never have become the person that I am today. In his case, gratitude required both acceptance and forgiveness. Although I ended my last book, *Breathe*, by telling him that I loved him, just before Christmas 2022, Rorion complained that I had falsely stated in *Breathe* that Royce never paid me for coaching him in the UFC.

I laughed out loud, shook my head, and cursed myself for not expecting this. Rorion is who he is and will never change. In the end, I agreed to add an "Editor's Note" to *Breathe* stating that our memories on this event differ. Life is too short to waste time and energy on such things. For me, forgiveness and freedom walk hand in hand. Anger takes energy and is corrosive to my psyche. Given my battle with Parkinson's, I have no room in my life for unnecessary conflict. This year on my birthday, Rorion came to my house to give me some papayas; I never mentioned this dispute.

Recently, Nobuhiko Takada came to my studio with a group of Japanese Jiu Jitsu students to learn Invisible Jiu Jitsu. Takada and I fought in 1997 and 1998, but this time he came to see me as a student. Although he was once Japan's Hulk Hogan, he impressed me with his humility and dedication to the martial art of Jiu Jitsu. He is a really nice guy. Takada has been training for a few years in Japan, is a decent purple belt, but still has lots of small details to learn. When I taught him about base, connection, breathing, and some of the invisible aspects of Jiu Jitsu, he was fascinated. Like most students today, nobody had ever taught him these things. He will be returning to California soon for more classes. After he left, I realized that our relationship had come full circle, and it made me feel very happy.

I recently heard that my old nemesis, King Zulu, could no longer walk and was in a wheelchair. He was supposed to have a hip operation, but there was no guarantee that he would ever walk again. This sad news struck a chord deep inside me. I called my friend Sergio "Malibu" Jardim and said, "We have to help Zulu!" Nobody tested me like King Zulu did in our first fight. He opened my eyes and changed the way I looked at fighting forever. Coming face-to-face with my worst nightmare was not only a sink-or-swim moment. King Zulu forced me to be present, accept my destiny, and realize that any battle could be my last. It was the most intense experience of my life.

I asked Malibu to find out how we could improve the quality of King Zulu's daily life and he called back a few days later and said, "King Zulu doesn't have a wheelchair ramp. It's a nightmare for him to get in and out of his house. He also has a hard time sleeping because his mattress is old and worn-out." First I had Malibu pay someone to go to King Zulu's house and build a wheelchair ramp. Now I'm raising the money to buy him a new mattress and an electric wheelchair. I feel really good about this, because we were once adversaries and now we are in similar shoes. We are both getting old and battling health problems; now I see him as a fellow human who needs help. Our bitter rivalry has transformed into friendship. I am very grateful for what he taught me. We have put the turbulent times behind us and have reached a more peaceful place. I am happy to have experienced all of it and can now be of service to him.

Today I love my opponents. Without them, I would not be who I am. While I have no mercy when I go into battle, I have love in my heart, because by fighting I am connected to my ancestors and God, expressing myself in the most complete possible way. My opponent is the least of my worries. Wherever I end up in the afterlife will be the same place as my father, son, brothers, cousins, and most of my opponents. The prospect of their ridicule is enough to dissuade me from ever taking the easy road.

Like my friend Winston said, Parkinson's is like having an unruly passenger sitting in your car. If you let him, he will grab the wheel and drive your car off the road. I feel like the changes in my medications, diet, lifestyle, and mindset have improved my day-to-day life. Parkinson's is no longer in the passenger seat; it is in the trunk. Occasionally I will hear a thump or two coming from the trunk. Usually I just turn up the radio, but if the fucker makes too much noise, I slam on the brakes and send him smashing into the back seat. It is important that Parkinson's disease remembers who is driving the car.

ACKNOWLEDGMENTS

First and foremost, I must thank my wife, Cassia, who has been an incredible pillar of love and support. I must also thank my father, Hélio Gracie; my brothers Rolls and Rorion Gracie; and my teacher, Orlando Cani, for all that they taught me. Without them, I would never have been able to achieve the things that I achieved. My dear son Rockson continues to inspire me to do my best until the end. Once again, my old friend (and *Breathe* coauthor), Peter Maguire, helped me articulate my ideas about Jiu Jitsu and life. Turnabout is fair play, so it is only fair that he pushed me as hard on my words and ideas as I've pushed him on the mat over the last three decades. I would also like to thank the doctors and scholars who taught Peter and me about biology, science, and physics, then offered valuable insights and read drafts of this book. Professor Wayland Tseh helped us better understand and describe breathing and the role oxygen plays in human performance. Physics professor and Jiu Jitsu student, Dylan McNamara, taught us about leverage and its role in Jiu Jitsu. Dr. Frank Snyder offered new insights into the role that dopamine plays in the brain. A special thanks goes to our editor, Peter Dimock, whose probing and sometimes painful questions improved both *Breathe* and this book. Thanks to Annabelle Lee Carter and Henryk Jaronowski for reading and editing numerous drafts of this book and greatly improving it. Thanks to Chris Burns for bringing this book to life with his illustrations. Last, but not least, our agent, Frank Weimann, deserves thanks for finding us a happy home at HarperCollins, and being our loyal supporter, advocate, and frontline soldier.

ABOUT THE AUTHORS

Rickson Gracie is the *New York Times* bestselling author of *Breathe*. The leader of the most prominent martial arts family of all time, Gracie reigned as world Jiu Jitsu champion in both the middle-heavyweight and open divisions for almost two decades. Since retiring with an undefeated record, he has focused on unifying and spreading his family martial art through his Jiu Jitsu Global Federation.

Peter Maguire is the author of *Law and War, Facing Death in Cambodia, Thai Stick*, and coauthor of *Breathe*. Maguire has taught the law and theory of war at Columbia University, Bard College, and University of North Carolina at Wilmington. He is the founder and director of Fainting Robin Foundation. Maguire received his black belt from Rickson Gracie and has been his friend and student for more than thirty years.